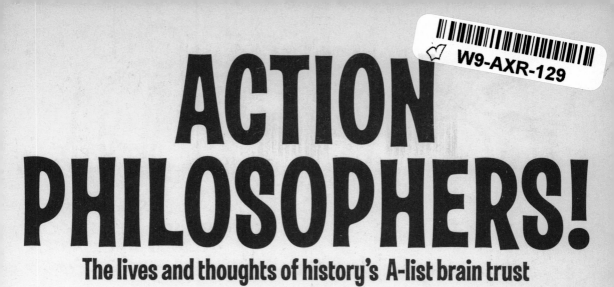

ACTION PHILOSOPHERS!

The lives and thoughts of history's A-list brain trust

VOLUME THREE

by Fred Van Lente and Ryan Dunlavey

ROLL CALL for ACTION!!

"PHILOSOPHY IS NOT A *THEORY*, BUT AN *ACTIVITY*."
--LUDWIG WITTGENSTEIN,
TRACTATUS LOGICO-PHILOSOPHICUS

ACTION PHILOSOPHERS GIANT-SIZE THING VOL. 3 IS PUBLISHED BY EVIL TWIN COMICS, 262 FIFTH AVENUE, 2ND FLOOR, BROOKLYN, NY, 11215. THE MATERIAL IN THE BOOK ORIGINALLY APPEARED IN PERIODICAL FORM IN *ACTION PHILOSOPHERS #7-9*. ALL CONTENTS ARE COPYRIGHT AND TRADEMARKED 2007 BY RYAN DUNLAVEY AND FRED VAN LENTE. ALL RIGHTS RESERVED. NO PART OF THIS PUBLICATION MAY BE REPRODUCED WITHOUT WRITTEN PERMISSION FROM THE COPYRIGHT HOLDERS. FIRST PRINTING: NOVEMBER 2007. PRINTED IN CANADA.

ISBN-10: 0-9778329-2-9
ISBN-13: 978-0-9778329-2-7

"OF THE *FIRST* PHILOSOPHERS," WRITES THE FIRST REAL *HISTORIAN* OF PHILOSOPHY, *ARISTOTLE*, "MOST THOUGHT THE PRINCIPLES WHICH WERE OF THE NATURE OF *MATTER* WERE THE *ONLY* PRINCIPLES OF *ALL* THINGS."

IN OTHER WORDS, THERE WERE NO "*META*"-PHYSICS... THE MATERIAL, IDEALISTIC, AND SPIRITUAL WORLDS ALL OBEYED *IDENTICAL* LAWS!

THESE THEORIES PREVAILED IN THE DAYS BEFORE THE FIRST *MEGA-STAR* PHILOSOPHER, *SOCRATES*, SO THE THINKERS THAT EXPOUNDED THEM ARE KNOWN, COLLECTIVELY, AS *ACTION PHILOSOPHER(S)* #19...

THE PRE-SOCRATICS!

THE FIRST PRINCIPLES OF THIS *COMIC BOOK* ARE STORY (BY *FRED VAN LENTE*) AND ART (BY *RYAN DUNLAVEY*)!

THALES of MILETUS!

ANAXIMANDER!

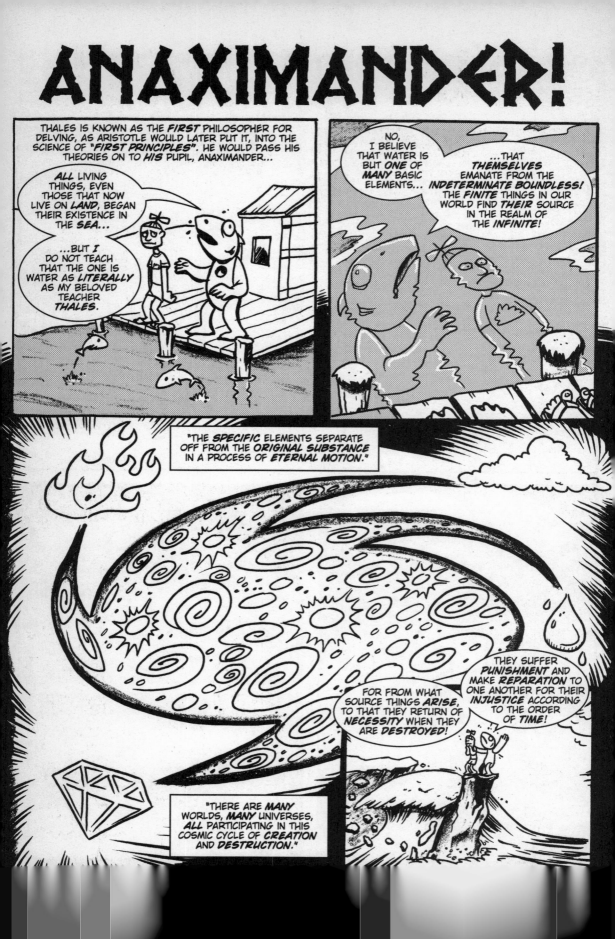

THALES IS KNOWN AS THE *FIRST* PHILOSOPHER FOR DELVING, AS ARISTOTLE WOULD LATER PUT IT, INTO THE SCIENCE OF *"FIRST PRINCIPLES"*. HE WOULD PASS HIS THEORIES ON TO *HIS* PUPIL, ANAXIMANDER...

ALL LIVING THINGS, EVEN THOSE THAT NOW LIVE ON *LAND*, BEGAN THEIR EXISTENCE IN THE *SEA*...

...BUT *I* DO NOT TEACH THAT THE ONE IS WATER AS *LITERALLY* AS MY BELOVED TEACHER *THALES*.

NO, I BELIEVE THAT WATER IS BUT *ONE* OF *MANY* BASIC ELEMENTS...

...THAT *THEMSELVES* EMANATE FROM THE *INDETERMINATE BOUNDLESS!* THE *FINITE* THINGS IN OUR WORLD FIND *THEIR* SOURCE IN THE REALM OF THE *INFINITE!*

"THE *SPECIFIC* ELEMENTS SEPARATE OFF FROM THE *ORIGINAL SUBSTANCE* IN A PROCESS OF *ETERNAL MOTION*."

FOR FROM WHAT SOURCE THINGS *ARISE*, TO THAT THEY RETURN OF *NECESSITY* WHEN THEY ARE *DESTROYED!*

THEY SUFFER *PUNISHMENT* AND MAKE *REPARATION* TO ONE ANOTHER FOR THEIR *INJUSTICE* ACCORDING TO THE ORDER OF *TIME!*

"THERE ARE *MANY* WORLDS, *MANY* UNIVERSES, *ALL* PARTICIPATING IN THIS COSMIC CYCLE OF *CREATION* AND *DESTRUCTION*."

ANAXIMENES!

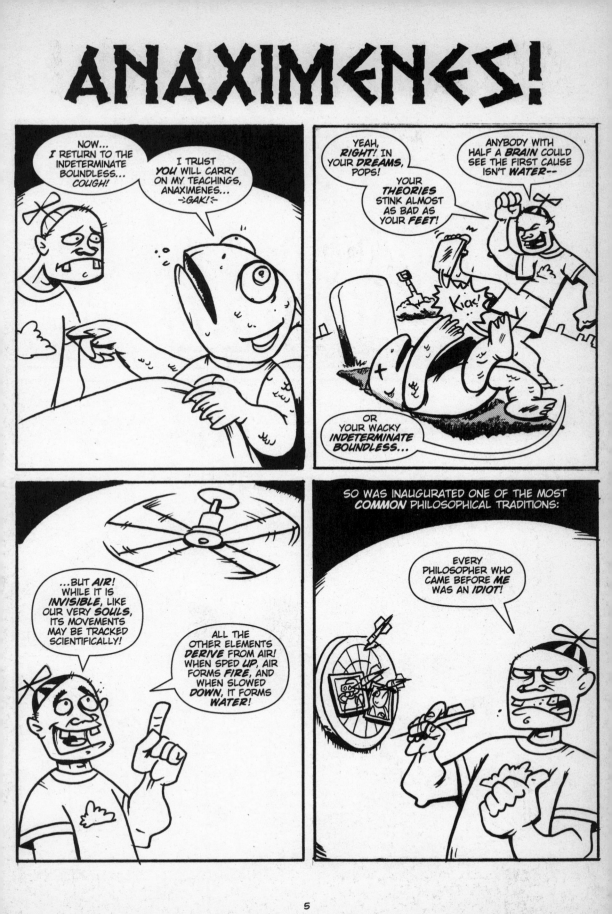

HERACLITUS!

THE WORLD IS, HERACLITUS SAYS, AN *"EVER-LIVING FIRE"* WHICH IS MAINTAINED BY "MEASURES OF IT *KINDLING* AND MEASURES GOING OUT."

"ALL THINGS ARE AN EXCHANGE FOR *FIRE*, AND FIRE FOR *ALL THINGS*, EVEN AS WARES FOR *GOLD* AND GOLD FOR *WARES*."

NOTHING IS EVER *DESTROYED*, BUT MERELY CONVERTS TO A DIFFERENT *FORM!* THIS NOTION IS REMARKABLY SIMILAR TO PHYSICS' NOTION OF THE CONSERVATION OF MATTER AND ENERGY.

OOOHHH... PRETTY...

HENCE WE HAVE *STABILITY* IN THE UNIVERSE NOT IN *SPITE* OF, BUT *BECAUSE* OF CONSTANT *CHANGE!*

GOD *IS* FIRE, AND GOD-FIRE PERMEATES *ALL* THINGS--INCLUDING THE HUMAN *SOUL!*

REASON IS THE *FIRE* OF THE SOUL, FOR ONLY THROUGH *IT* CAN WE SEE THAT WHICH IS SHARED BY ALL *THINGS!*

THUS, THOUGH MEN ARE ALL *DIFFERENT*, THEY ARE *UNITED* BY A *SINGLE* FLAME!

AND THOUGH MEN ALWAYS *DISAGREE*, "WHAT IS IN *OPPOSITION* IS IN *CONCERT* AND FROM WHAT *DIFFERS* COMES THE MOST BEAUTIFUL *HARMONY*."

JUST AS *FIRE* IS THE CONSTANT IN *CHANGE*, IT IS ONLY THROUGH THE TENSION BETWEEN *OPPOSITES* THAT THE UNIVERSE ACHIEVES *ORDER!*

PARMENIDES!

EMPEDOCLES!

LEGEND HAS IT EMPEDOCLES WANTED TO BE REMEMBERED AS A *GOD*, SO HE LEAPT INTO THE VOLCANO AT *MT. ETNA* TO ERASE ALL TRACE OF HIS *BODY*.

WHY CAN'T PHILOSOPHERS JUST GET *ALONG*?

I FIGURED OUT A WAY *NONE* OF US CAN BE WRONG!

PARMENIDES WAS CORRECT WHEN HE SAID WHAT *IS* ALWAYS *WAS*;

BUT HERACLITUS WAS RIGHT *TOO* THAT WITH *CHANGE* THE UNIVERSE IS ALWAYS *ABUZZ*!

I SAY IT'S THE *ELEMENTS* THAT MAKE *UP* THE *ONE* THAT ARE ALWAYS IN *FLUX*.

THALES SAID IT WAS *WATER*, ANAXIMENES SAID IT WAS *AIR*... I SAY THEY'RE *BOTH* RIGHT, THE BRAINY YOUNG BUCKS!

WIND AND WATER ARE BUT *TWO* OF THE *FOUR* THAT MAKE UP ALL THE WORLD'S *MATTER*. *FIRE* AND *EARTH* ROUND OUT THAT QUARTET--

--AND THUS ENDS MY PHILOSOPHICAL PATTER!

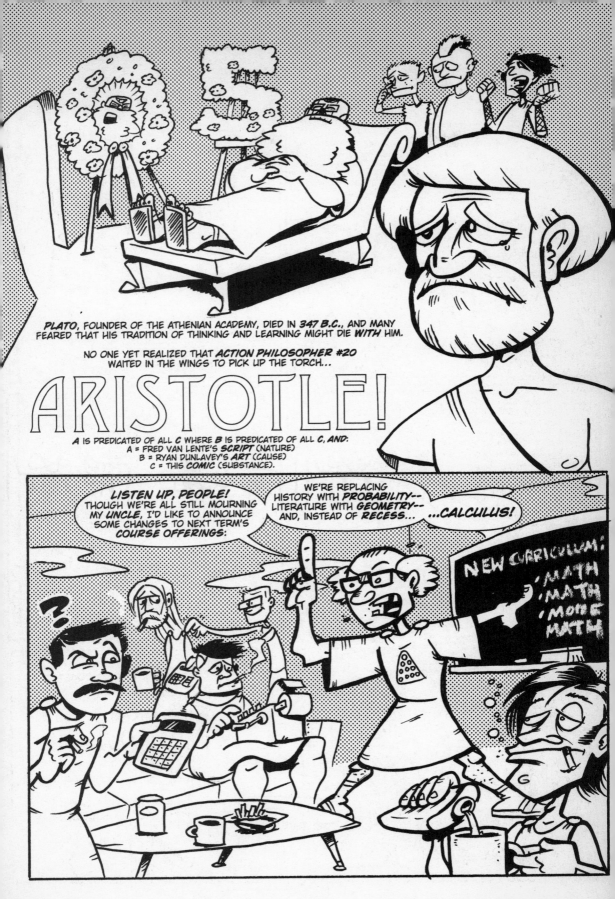

PLATO, FOUNDER OF THE ATHENIAN ACADEMY, DIED IN *347 B.C.*, AND MANY FEARED THAT HIS TRADITION OF THINKING AND LEARNING MIGHT DIE *WITH HIM.*

NO ONE YET REALIZED THAT *ACTION PHILOSOPHER #20* WAITED IN THE WINGS TO PICK UP THE TORCH...

ARISTOTLE!

A IS PREDICATED OF ALL *C* WHERE *B* IS PREDICATED OF ALL *C*, *AND:*
A = FRED VAN LENTE'S *SCRIPT* (NATURE)
B = RYAN DUNLAVEY'S *ART* (CAUSE)
C = THIS *COMIC* (SUBSTANCE).

LISTEN UP, *PEOPLE!* THOUGH WE'RE ALL STILL MOURNING MY *UNCLE*, I'D LIKE TO ANNOUNCE SOME CHANGES TO NEXT TERM'S *COURSE OFFERINGS:*

WE'RE REPLACING HISTORY WITH *PROBABILITY*-- LITERATURE WITH *GEOMETRY*-- AND, INSTEAD OF *RECESS...*

...CALCULUS!

NEW CURRICULUM: • MATH • MATH • MORE MATH

SEE HERE, SPEUSIPPUS! I KNOW PLATO NAMED YOU HIS *SUCCESSOR*...

...BUT I'VE TAUGHT *BIOLOGY* AT THIS SCHOOL FOR ALMOST *TWENTY YEARS*! I DON'T SEE IT OFFERED *ANYWHERE* IN YOUR NEW COURSE CATALOG!

I *KNOW* WHO YOU ARE, ARISTOTLE...

...I ALSO KNOW YOU NEVER APPRECIATED THE *MATHEMATICAL BEAUTY* OF MY UNCLE'S THEORY OF *FORMS*!

WELL...*YES*, I PROTESTED HIS IDEA THAT THE FORMS ACTUALLY *EXIST* IN NATURE, THOUGH THERE IS NO *EMPIRICAL EVIDENCE* TO SUSTAIN SUCH A CLAIM--

-:TSK!:- A *PITY*.

SAY, THAT *REMINDS* ME--WE'VE *REPLACED* BIOLOGY WITH *ACCOUNTING*!

IF YOU DON'T *LIKE* IT, I BELIEVE THERE'S A *HALL MONITOR* POSITION OPEN...

SON OF THE ROYAL PHYSICIAN TO THE COURT OF NEARBY *MACEDON*, ARISTOTLE HAD ARRIVED AT THE ACADEMY AS A 17-YEAR-OLD STUDENT AND NEVER *LEFT*...

SEE IF YOU CAN'T ADD *THIS* UP, SPEUSIPPUS...

...I *QUIT*!

...UNTIL *NOW*!

UNLIKE PLATO, HE BELIEVED THAT BEING WASN'T *STATIC*, BUT RATHER IN A CONSTANT STATE OF *CHANGE*--SO ONE COULD DRAW CONCLUSIONS ABOUT IT ONLY BY *OBSERVING* BEINGS IN ACTION IN NATURE.

AFTER LEAVING THE *ACADEMY*, HE EMBARKED ON A SERIES OF TEACHING GIGS AND SCIENTIFIC EXPEDITIONS TO VARIOUS PLACES AROUND THE HELLENIC WORLD, INCLUDING THE ISLAND OF *LESBOS*.

WHAT'S *HER* PROBLEM?

THEN, IN 343 B.C., HE RECEIVED A *ROYAL SUMMONS* FROM MACEDON'S *KING PHILIP II*:

YOU SHALL COME *TUTOR* THE *HEIR* TO THE THRONE!

OH, WELL. I GUESS A STEADY PAYCHECK *WOULD* SUPPORT MY *RESEARCH*...

12

13

14

ART ARISES WHEN FROM MANY NOTIONS GAINED BY EXPERIENCE ONE UNIVERSAL JUDGMENT ABOUT A CLASS OF OBJECTS IS PRODUCED.

TO SAY WHEN YOUR FRIEND CALLIAS WAS ILL OF THIS DISEASE AND THIS MEDICINE DID HIM GOOD, THAT IS EXPERIENCE--

--BUT TO SAY THE SAME MEDICINE WILL DO GOOD TO ALL MEN WITH THAT DISEASE, THAT IS ART!

FOR MEN OF EXPERIENCE MAY KNOW THAT A THING IS SO, BUT NOT KNOW WHY.

HENCE WE THINK THAT MASTER-WORKERS IN EACH CRAFT ARE WISER THAN THE MANUAL WORKERS, FOR THEY KNOW THE CAUSES OF THE THINGS THAT ARE DONE.

FURTHERMORE, ARTISTS, BECAUSE THEY KNOW THE WHYS OF A THING, UNLIKE MEN OF MERE EXPERIENCE, MAY TEACH OTHERS HOW TO DO IT.

A LOT OF TIMES, THAT'S THE ONLY WORK THEY CAN GET!

I HEARD THAT!

SO...THE MAN OF EXPERIENCE IS SMARTER THAN THOSE THAT MERELY POSSESS SENSE PERCEPTION...

...THE ARTIST SMARTER THAN THE MAN OF EXPERIENCE, THE MASTER-WORKER THAN THE MECHANIC...

...BUT, IF I AM TO BE KING, I NEED TO BE SMARTER THAN ALL OF THEM COMBINED, MASTER!

AAAGGH!!
IN THE CASE OF A HOTFOOT... BECAUSE IT'S FREAKIN' HILARIOUS! HA HA!!
GRRRRR!! JUST AS IN REGULAR PHYSICS, THE BASIS OF ALL METAPHYSICS IS MOTION--
--FOR CHANGE ("KINESIS") IS THE ONLY CONSTANT IN NATURE!
AND THE MOST COMMON FORM OF CHANGE-- THE ONE NECESSARY TO EXISTENCE--
--IS WHEN BEINGS MOVE FROM A POTENTIAL STATE--
--SUCH AS AN ACORN IS A POTENTIAL TREE, OR A PILE OF LUMBER & BRICKS IS A POTENTIAL HOUSE--
--OR ME PREPARING TO WRING YOUR NECK--
--TO AN ACTUAL STATE!
SNOT-NOSED--LITTLE--ROYAL--PUNK! SET ME ON FIRE, WILLYA--
GAK!
CHOKE!
ARISTOTLE! HOW GOES THE BOY'S FIRST DAY OF STUDY?
KING PHILIP! AH... WELL...
GASP! WHEEZE!

19

YEARS PASSED THIS WAY, BUT ALEXANDER'S SCHOOLING FINALLY CAME TO AN *ABRUPT END* UPON HIS FATHER'S *ASSASSINATION* IN 336 B.C., NECESSITATING THE PRINCE'S *CORONATION.*

MY ARMIES AND I MARCH EAST TO *PERSIA,* MASTER. WOULD YOU COME *WITH* ME, SO I MIGHT CONTINUE TO BENEFIT FROM YOUR WISE COUNSEL?

THANK YOU, ALE--

YOUR *MAJESTY,* I MEAN! ->HEH!<- BUT NO...

"...I HAVE RESOLVED TO RETURN TO *ATHENS*...AND USE THE MONEY I EARNED *HERE* TO BUY LAND FOR MY *OWN* SCHOOL!"

SOCRATES *HIMSELF* CAME TO THINK UNDER THESE GROVES--SACRED AS THEY ARE TO APOLLO LYCEUS, THE *LIGHT-GIVER!*

OOH! GOOD *KARMA!* I'LL *TAKE* IT!

ARISTOTLE'S *LYCEUM* OPENED AROUND 334 B.C. HIS UNUSUAL TEACHING METHOD INVOLVED WALKING AROUND A *PERIPATOS,* OR COVERED WALK...SO HIS SCHOOL WAS CALLED *"PERIPATETIC."*

MASTER, YOU'VE RECEIVED A LETTER FROM YOUR FORMER *PUPIL,* THE KING OF *MACEDON!*

READ IT TO ME, WILL YOU?

Dear Master,

Having a *smashing time* conquering Asia Minor. And I do mean that *literally!* Ha, ha!

But *seriously,* in my campaigns I have come across many fascinating *specimens* that will help you in your *research.* I will be sending them to you shortly.

Whoops— The ground is *shaking,* so that must mean enemy *war elephants* are on their way! No rest for the *wicked!*

Hope the Lyceum is going well and I will write again soon.

XOXOXOXOX ALEX.

ACTION PHILOSOPHER #21:
EPICTETUS THE STOIC!

THIS PHILOSOPHER'S REAL NAME REMAINS *UNKNOWN* -- "EPICTETUS" SIMPLY MEANS "*SLAVE*".

HIS ROMAN MASTER ALLOWED HIM TO BE TUTORED IN A SCHOOL OF THOUGHT DEVELOPED BY *ZENO OF CITIUM*, A CITY ON THE SOUTHEAST COAST OF WHAT IS NOW *CYPRUS*.

THIS PHILOSOPHY GOT ITS NAME FROM ZENO'S HABIT OF HANGING OUT IN THE *STOA*, OR PORTICOS OF BUILDINGS.

WRITER: FRED VAN LENTE
ARTIST: RYAN DUNLAVEY*

*: BUT IT'S NOT LIKE WE'RE *PROUD* OF IT OR ANYTHING.**

**: WE'RE NOT *ASHAMED*, EITHER...

DIOGENES LAERTES WRITES THAT THE STOICS THOUGHT OF PHILOSOPHY LIKE AN *EGG*:

"THE SHELL IS *LOGIC*, NEXT COMES THE WHITE, *ETHICS*, AND THE YOLK IN THE CENTER IS *PHYSICS*."

ALL STOIC *PHYSICAL* THEORY RETURNS TO THE IDEA THAT GOD IS *IN ALL THINGS*.

THERE ARE TWO PRINCIPLES FOR THE UNIVERSE, THE *ACTIVE* AND THE *PASSIVE*.

NEW GOD

GODYEAR

GOD
GOD ST.
GOD
GOD
GOD TIMES

MATTER IS THE *PASSIVE* FORM OF *GOD* AND GOD IS THE *ACTIVE* FORM OF *MATTER*.

THE ROMAN STOIC *SENECA* WROTE:

WHY SHOULD YOU NOT BELIEVE THAT SOMETHING OF *DIVINITY* EXISTS IN ONE WHO IS PART OF *GOD*?

THE WHOLE UNIVERSE THAT CONTAINS US IS ONE, AND IS *GOD*; WE ARE HIS ASSOCIATES AND HIS *MEMBERS*.

GOD

ZENO HIMSELF USES *THIS* ANALOGY:

"IF *PLANE TREES* BORE *LYRES* RESOUNDING MELODIOUSLY, YOU WOULD ALSO NATURALLY THINK THAT *MUSIC* EXISTED IN *PLANE TREES*."

"WHY, THEREFORE, IS THE *WORLD* NOT CONSIDERED *ANIMATE* AND INTELLIGENT, WHEN IT PRODUCES FROM *ITSELF* ANIMATE AND INTELLIGENT *BEINGS*?"

THEREFORE *NOTHING*, AS PLUTARCH SAYS, "EITHER RESTS OR IS MOVED OTHERWISE THAN ACCORDING TO THE REASON OF *GOD*, WHICH IS THE SAME THING AS *FATE*."

LITTLE WONDER THAT SUCH A *FATALISTIC* OUTLOOK ATTRACTED ADHERENTS AMONG *SLAVES*...

...BUT OUR NAMELESS HERO WANTED TO *CONTINUE* TO PREACH STOICISM IN ROME EVEN *AFTER* HE BOUGHT HIS *FREEDOM*!

UNFORTUNATELY FOR *HIM*, THE PARANOID EMPEROR *DOMITIAN EXILED* ALL PHILOSOPHERS FROM THE IMPERIAL CAPITAL IN A.D. 94.

AND *STAY* OUT!

24

EPICTETUS WOUND UP IN GREECE, SPECIFICALLY *EPIRUS*, & WHERE HIS TEACHINGS REALLY BEGAN TO *CATCH ON*.

AFTER HE DIED AROUND 127, HIS STUDENT *FLAVIUS ARRIAN* ASSEMBLED HIS TEACHINGS INTO EIGHT *DISCOURSES*--

NO LOITERING

--THE *ETHICAL* PARTS OF WHICH ARRIAN CONDENSED INTO THE *ENCHIRIDION (MANUAL)*, WHICH FAMOUSLY BEGINS:

OF ALL EXISTING THINGS, SOME ARE *IN* OUR POWER, AND OTHERS ARE *NOT* IN OUR POWER.

IN OUR POWER ARE THOUGHT, IMPULSE, WILL TO *GET* AND WILL TO *AVOID*...

...IN A WORD, EVERYTHING WHICH *IS* OUR OWN DOING.

THINGS IN OUR POWER ARE BY NATURE *FREE*, UNHINDERED, UNTRAMMELED.

THINGS *NOT* IN OUR POWER INCLUDE THE BODY, PROPERTY, REPUTATION, OFFICE...

...IN A WORD, EVERYTHING WHICH IS *NOT* OUR OWN DOING.

THINGS *NOT* IN OUR POWER ARE WEAK, SERVILE, SUBJECT TO HINDRANCE, DEPENDENT ON OTHERS.

REMEMBER THEN THAT IF YOU IMAGINE WHAT IS NATURALLY *SLAVISH* IS FREE, AND WHAT IS NATURALLY ANOTHER'S IS *YOUR OWN*...

...YOU WILL BE *HAMPERED*, YOU WILL MOURN, YOU WILL BE PUT TO *CONFUSION*, YOU WILL BLAME GODS AND MEN.

GATE 13

TERRORISM

BUT IF YOU THINK THAT ONLY YOUR OWN BELONGS TO YOU, AND THAT WHAT IS ANOTHER'S IS INDEED ANOTHER'S....

NO ONE WILL HARM YOU, YOU WILL HAVE NO ENEMY, FOR NO HARM CAN *TOUCH* YOU.

ZZZ

AIMING THEN AT THESE *LOFTY MATTERS*, YOU MUST REMEMBER THAT TO *ATTAIN* THEM REQUIRES MORE THAN *ORDINARY* EFFORT.

YOU WILL HAVE TO GIVE UP SOME THINGS ENTIRELY, AND PUT OTHERS *OFF* FOR THE MOMENT.

AND IF YOU WOULD HAVE STATUS AND WEALTH, YOU MAY *FAIL* TO GET THEM, JUST BECAUSE YOUR DESIRE IS SET ON THE *FORMER*...

...AND YOU WILL *CERTAINLY* FAIL TO ATTAIN THOSE THINGS WHICH ALONE BRING FREEDOM AND *HAPPINESS*.

MAKE IT YOUR STUDY THEN TO CONFRONT *EVERY* HARSH IMPRESSION WITH THE WORDS:

YOU ARE BUT AN *IMPRESSION*, AND NOT AT ALL WHAT YOU *SEEM TO BE*.

THEN *TEST IT* BY THOSE RULES THAT YOU POSSESS; AND FIRST BY *THIS*:

ARE YOU CONCERNED WITH WHAT *IS* IN MY POWER OR WITH WHAT IS *NOT* IN MY POWER?

AND IF IT IS CONCERNED WITH WHAT IS *NOT* IN YOUR POWER..

I HAVE NO CONTROL OVER WHAT *EVIL PEOPLE* MIGHT DO!

...BE READY WITH THE ANSWER THAT IT IS *NOTHING* TO YOU.

CURSES! LOST *ANOTHER* ONE!

WHAT TROUBLES MEN ARE NOT *THINGS*, BUT RATHER THE JUDGMENTS THEY MAKE *ABOUT* THINGS.

FOR EXAMPLE, *DEATH HAS NOTHING* ABOUT IT TO BE FEARED, OR ELSE IT WOULD HAVE APPEARED FEARFUL TO SOCRATES.

BUT THE *JUDGMENT THAT* DEATH HAS SOMETHING FEARFUL ABOUT IT--*THAT* IS WHAT IS FEARFUL.

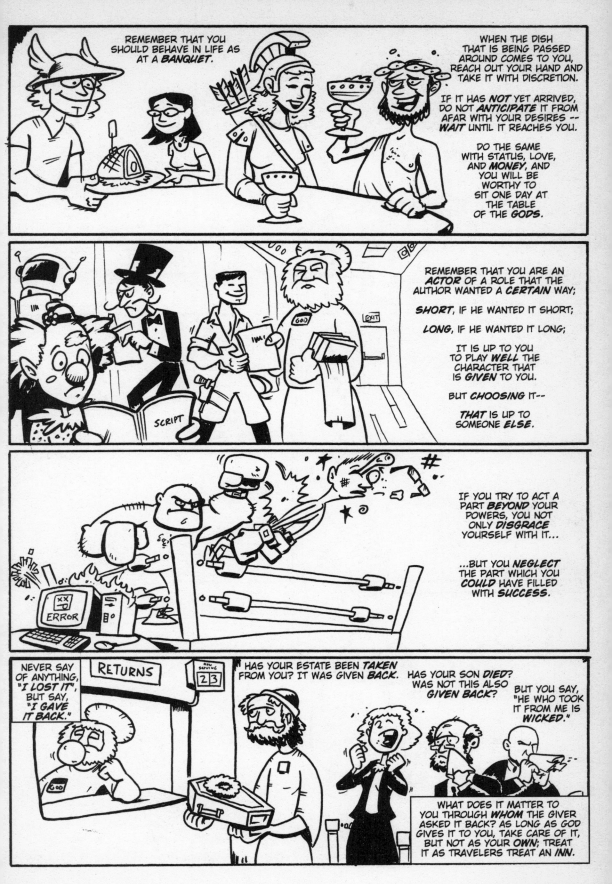

REMEMBER THAT YOU SHOULD BEHAVE IN LIFE AS AT A *BANQUET*.

WHEN THE DISH THAT IS BEING PASSED AROUND COMES TO YOU, REACH OUT YOUR HAND AND TAKE IT WITH DISCRETION.

IF IT HAS *NOT* YET ARRIVED, DO NOT *ANTICIPATE* IT FROM AFAR WITH YOUR DESIRES -- *WAIT* UNTIL IT REACHES YOU.

DO THE SAME WITH STATUS, LOVE, AND *MONEY*, AND YOU WILL BE WORTHY TO SIT ONE DAY AT THE TABLE OF THE *GODS*.

REMEMBER THAT YOU ARE AN *ACTOR* OF A ROLE THAT THE AUTHOR WANTED A *CERTAIN* WAY;

SHORT, IF HE WANTED IT SHORT;

LONG, IF HE WANTED IT LONG;

IT IS UP TO YOU TO PLAY *WELL* THE CHARACTER THAT IS *GIVEN* TO YOU.

BUT *CHOOSING* IT--

THAT IS UP TO SOMEONE *ELSE*.

SCRIPT

IF YOU TRY TO ACT A PART *BEYOND* YOUR POWERS, YOU NOT ONLY *DISGRACE* YOURSELF WITH IT...

...BUT YOU *NEGLECT* THE PART WHICH YOU *COULD* HAVE FILLED WITH *SUCCESS*.

ERROR

NEVER SAY OF ANYTHING, "*I LOST IT*", BUT SAY, "*I GAVE IT BACK*."

RETURNS

HAS YOUR ESTATE BEEN *TAKEN* FROM YOU? IT WAS GIVEN *BACK*.

HAS YOUR SON *DIED*? WAS NOT THIS ALSO *GIVEN BACK*?

BUT YOU SAY, "HE WHO TOOK IT FROM ME IS *WICKED*."

WHAT DOES IT MATTER TO YOU THROUGH *WHOM* THE GIVER ASKED IT BACK? AS LONG AS GOD GIVES IT TO YOU, TAKE CARE OF IT, BUT NOT AS YOUR *OWN*; TREAT IT AS TRAVELERS TREAT AN *INN*.

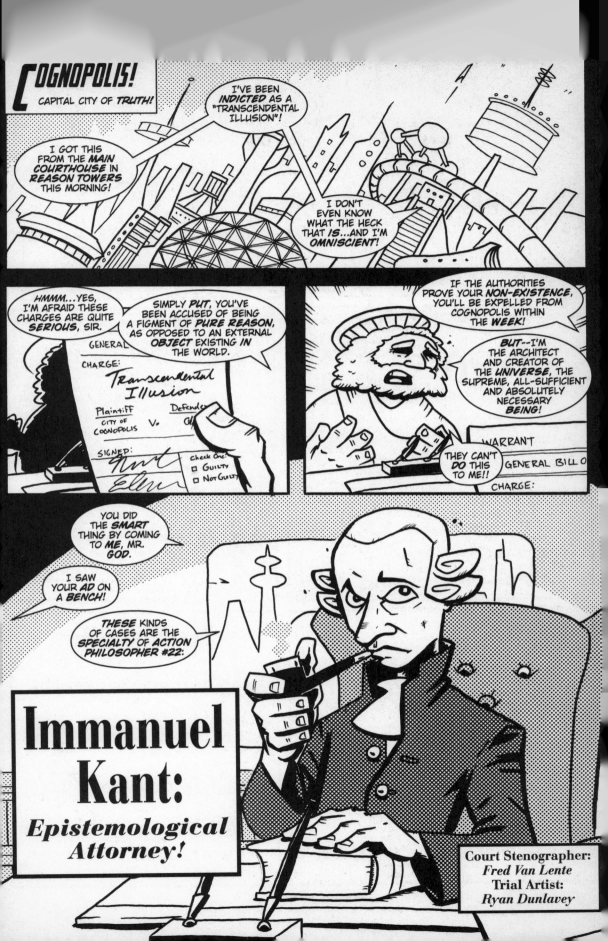

Court Stenographer:
Fred Van Lente
Trial Artist:
Ryan Dunlavey

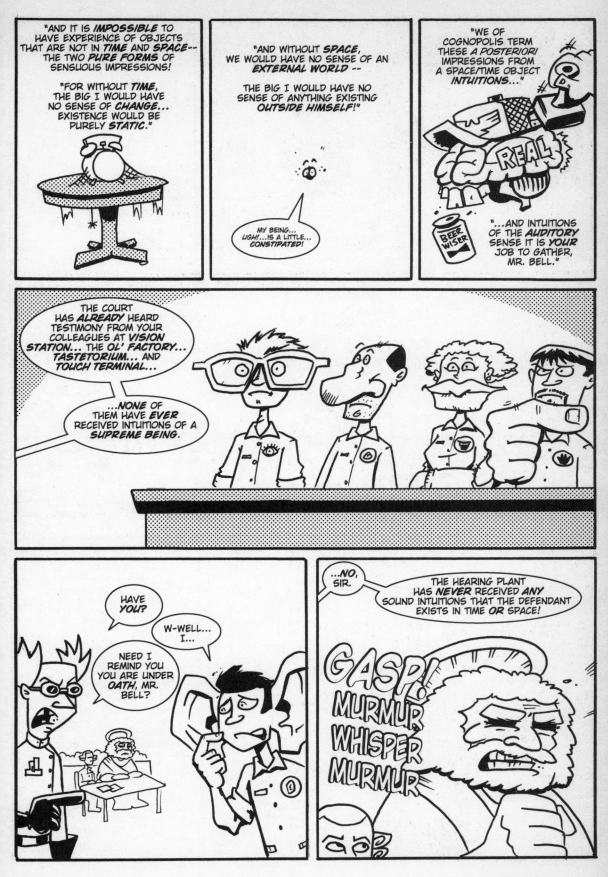

"AND IT IS *IMPOSSIBLE* TO HAVE EXPERIENCE OF OBJECTS THAT ARE NOT IN *TIME* AND *SPACE*-- THE TWO *PURE FORMS* OF SENSUOUS IMPRESSIONS!"

"FOR WITHOUT *TIME*, THE BIG I WOULD HAVE NO SENSE OF *CHANGE*... EXISTENCE WOULD BE PURELY *STATIC*."

"AND WITHOUT *SPACE*, WE WOULD HAVE NO SENSE OF AN *EXTERNAL WORLD* --

THE BIG I WOULD HAVE NO SENSE OF ANYTHING EXISTING *OUTSIDE* HIMSELF!"

MY BEING... UGH!...IS A LITTLE... CONSTIPATED!

"WE OF COGNOPOLIS TERM THESE *A POSTERIORI* IMPRESSIONS FROM A SPACE/TIME OBJECT *INTUITIONS*..."

REAL

BEER WISER

"...AND INTUITIONS OF THE *AUDITORY* SENSE IT IS *YOUR* JOB TO GATHER, MR. BELL."

THE COURT HAS *ALREADY* HEARD TESTIMONY FROM YOUR COLLEAGUES AT *VISION STATION*... THE OL' *FACTORY*... *TASTETORIUM*... AND *TOUCH TERMINAL*...

...*NONE* OF THEM HAVE *EVER* RECEIVED INTUITIONS OF A *SUPREME BEING*.

HAVE *YOU*?

W-WELL... I...

NEED I REMIND YOU YOU ARE UNDER *OATH*, MR. BELL?

...*NO*, SIR.

THE HEARING PLANT HAS *NEVER* RECEIVED *ANY* SOUND INTUITIONS THAT THE DEFENDANT EXISTS IN TIME *OR* SPACE!

GASP!
MURMUR
WHISPER
MURMUR

NOW THAT I MAY PROCEED →AHEM!← UNINTERRUPTED...

...I'D LIKE TO DRAW YOUR ATTENTION TO THE COSMOLOGICAL PROOF OF THE DEFENDANT'S EXISTENCE, DOCTOR.

"IN THIS TIDY BIT OF SOPHISTRY, IT IS ASSERTED THAT BECAUSE THE BIG I EXISTS, GOD MUST EXIST BY THE LAW OF CAUSE-AND-EFFECT...

THAT WITHOUT A NECESSARY BEING TO SET EXISTENCE IN MOTION IN THE FIRST PLACE, NOTHING WOULD EXIST AT ALL!"

"HOW WOULD YOU RESPOND?"

THE LAW OF CAUSE-AND-EFFECT IS A RATHER STICKY WICKET FOR PROFESSIONALS IN MY FIELD, SIR.

FOR ONE THING, IT IS IMPOSSIBLE TO PROVE EMPIRICALLY...

...BUT WITHOUT IT, EMPIRICAL EXPERIENCE COULD NOT EXIST!

HOW IS THAT POSSIBLE, DOCTOR?

"CAUSALITY CANNOT BE OBSERVED, AND THEREFORE CANNOT BE PART OF EMPIRICAL EXPERIENCE."

"WE ALL 'KNOW', FOR EXAMPLE, THAT WHEN YOU FREEZE WATER, IT TURNS TO ICE, YES?"

"BUT WHY? HAVE YOU EVER SEEN WATER FREEZE?"

GEEZ... THIS IS BORING... →YAWN!←

"OF COURSE NOT...YOU JUST GO AWAY, AND WHEN YOU COME BACK, IT'S ICE! THAT ESTABLISHES NO DEFINITIVE CAUSAL RELATIONSHIP--"

--NOR CAN YOU ESTABLISH ONE THROUGH THE SENSES ALONE!

MAY IT PLEASE THE COURT... PEOPLE'S EXHIBIT "A"!

A TABLE OF THE A PRIORI CONCEPTIONS OF THE UNDERSTANDING... THE CATEGORIES!

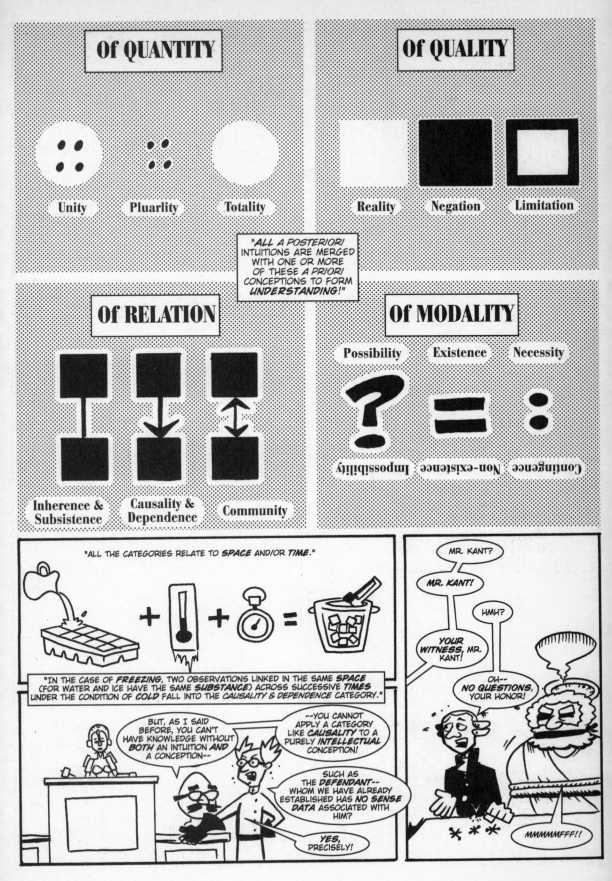

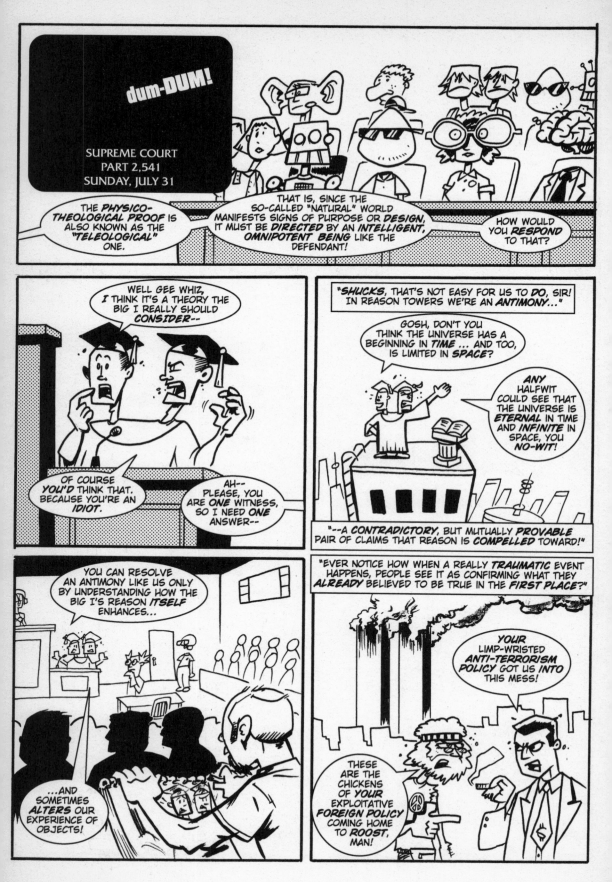

36

THAT'S BECAUSE, UNLESS WE'RE VIGILANT TO STOP IT, OUR REASON CAN IMPOSE *ARTIFICIAL PATTERNS* ON INCOMING DATA IN A MISGUIDED ATTEMPT TO RENDER THE *EXTERNAL* WORLD AS ORDERLY AS OUR *INTERNAL* ONE!

TAKE *CONSPIRACY THEORY*, FOR INSTANCE. THE POPULAR ON-LINE DOCUMENTARY *LOOSE CHANGE* (LOOSECHANGE911.COM) CONTENDS THAT THESE *SINISTER-SEEMING* FACTS FORM A *DAMNING PATTERN*:

IN SEPTEMBER 2000, CONSERVATIVE THINK TANK *PROJECT FOR A NEW AMERICAN CENTURY* (WHOSE MEMBERS INCLUDE *DICK CHENEY, DONALD RUMSFELD, JEB BUSH,* AND OTHER *BUSHIES*) WRITE THAT *"ANOTHER PEARL HARBOR"* IS NECESSARY TO REBUILD AMERICA'S DEFENSES.

EVIL PLANS 2000-2050

THAT *OCTOBER*, THE PENTAGON SIMULATES A BOEING 757 SMASHING INTO A *BUILDING.*

AND LESS THAN FOUR MONTHS PRIOR TO 9/11, THE OWNER OF THE TWIN TOWERS TOOK OUT A $3.5 BILLION TERRORISM *INSURANCE POLICY* ON THE W.T.C.!

AL-QUEDA INSURANCE CO. POLICY

BUT NEW AMERICAN CENTURY NEVER SAID AMERICA NEEDED TO *ENGINEER* SUCH AN ATTACK IN ORDER TO REJIGGER THE MILITARY!

UM...HEY...DOESN'T THE MILITARY HAVE, LIKE, *MISSILES* AND *BOMBS* AND STUFF TO KNOCK DOWN BUILDINGS? WOULDN'T THEY SIMULATE A CRASH JUST TO TRAIN *RESPONSES* TO IT?

SINCE TERRORISTS HAD ALREADY *TRIED* TO BLOW UP THE W.T.C. IN *1993*, DON'T YOU THINK GETTING INSURANCE OUT AGAINST IT HAPPENING *AGAIN* IS A PRETTY GOOD IDEA?

SO... IT IS *YOUR* CONTENTION THAT *"INTELLIGENT DESIGN"* IS CUT FROM THE SAME CLOTH AS *CONSPIRACY THEORY*: ANOTHER EXAMPLE OF REASON'S TENDENCY TO *OVERREACH*--TO MAKE *CONNECTIONS* WHERE THERE *ARE NONE*?

THAT'S SOMETHING WE *BOTH* CAN AGREE ON!

38

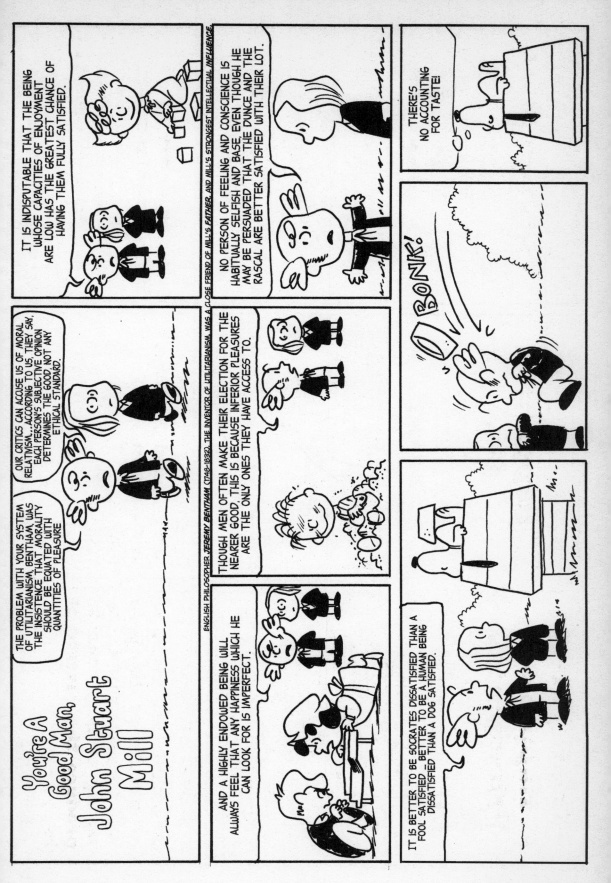

You're A
Good Man,
John Stuart
Mill

IT IS INDISPUTABLE THAT THE BEING WHOSE CAPACITIES OF ENJOYMENT ARE LOW HAS THE GREATEST CHANCE OF HAVING THEM FULLY SATISFIED.

NO PERSON OF FEELING AND CONSCIENCE IS HABITUALLY SELFISH AND BASE, EVEN THOUGH HE MAY BE PERSUADED THAT THE DUNCE AND THE RASCAL ARE BETTER SATISFIED WITH THEIR LOT.

THERE'S NO ACCOUNTING FOR TASTE!

BONK!

THE PROBLEM WITH YOUR SYSTEM OF UTILITARIANISM, BENTHAM, WAS THE INSISTENCE THAT MORALITY SHOULD BE EQUATED WITH QUANTITIES OF PLEASURE

OUR CRITICS CAN ACCUSE US OF MORAL RELATIVISM...ACCORDING TO US, THEY SAY, EACH PERSON'S SUBJECTIVE OPINION DETERMINES THE GOOD, NOT ANY ETHICAL STANDARD.

THOUGH MEN OFTEN MAKE THEIR ELECTION FOR THE NEARER GOOD, THIS IS BECAUSE INFERIOR PLEASURES ARE THE ONLY ONES THEY HAVE ACCESS TO.

ENGLISH PHILOSOPHER *JEREMY BENTHAM* (1748-1832), THE INVENTOR OF UTILITARIANISM, WAS A CLOSE FRIEND OF MILL'S *FATHER*, AND MILL'S STRONGEST INTELLECTUAL *INFLUENCE*.

AND A HIGHLY ENDOWED BEING WILL ALWAYS FEEL THAT ANY HAPPINESS WHICH HE CAN LOOK FOR IS IMPERFECT.

IT IS BETTER TO BE SOCRATES DISSATISFIED THAN A FOOL SATISFIED ... BETTER TO BE A HUMAN BEING DISSATISFIED THAN A DOG SATISFIED.

47

You're A Good Man, John Stuart Mill

50

Once upon a time...
(the 1820's)

...in a school far, far away...
(the University of Berlin)

There lived two professors...

GEORG W. F. HEGEL
(Action Philosopher #24)

ARTHUR SCHOPENHAUER
(Action Philosopher #25)

KANT

...and they BOTH thought

IMMANUEL KANT

was the greatest philosopher EVER!

SYNTHESIS (COMIC) = *THESIS* (FRED VAN LENTE) + *ANTITHESIS* (RYAN DUNLAVEY) **or** *WORLD* (COMIC) = *IDEA* (FRED VAN LENTE) + *REPRESENTATION* (RYAN DUNLAVEY)

Nevertheless, they BOTH disagreed with Kant's assertion that Things-in-THEMSELVES were fundamentally UNKNOWABLE.

From there, however...

Their paths RADICALLY DIVERGED...

ARTHUR REACHED *HIS* CONCLUSIONS...

...BECAUSE THE *PRINCIPLE OF SUFFICIENT REASON* SHOWS US THAT EVERYWHERE IS PRESENT *NECESSITY!*

TO HAVE PHYSICAL OBJECTS, A/K/A *PHENOMENA*, YOU NEED *CAUSE-AND-EFFECT!*

ABSTRACT CONCEPTS DEMAND INFERENCE OR *IMPLICATION!*

FREEDOM

MATH REQUIRES *TIME* (WITHOUT *SEQUENCE* YOU CAN'T *COUNT*)...

...AND *SPACE* (FOR *GEOMETRY*)!

"AND FOR THERE TO BE A *SELF*, THERE NEEDS TO BE AN ASPECT OF YOU THAT *YOU* OBSERVE ... AN *OBJECT*-YOU TO GO WITH THE *SUBJECT*-YOU!"

WILLING Subject

No-FRIEND SEX-BOX '720

KNOWING Subject

"THE SELF IS THE SUBJECT THAT *WILLS* AND THE *WILLING SUBJECT* IS THE OBJECT FOR THAT *KNOWING* SUBJECT!"

EVERYTHING IN THE WORLD (INCLUDING *YOU*) IS PRESENTED TO YOUR MIND AS AN *OBJECT* TO A *SUBJECT.*

ARTHUR CONCLUDES, "THE WHOLE WORLD OF OBJECTS IS AND REMAINS *REPRESENTATION*, AND THEREFORE WHOLLY AND FOREVER DETERMINED BY THE *SUBJECT*."

HENCE THE TITLE OF ARTHUR'S MOST FAMOUS WORK:

No-FRIEND SEX-BOX '72

THE WORLD AS WILL AND REPRESENTATION.*

*: *"VORSTELLUNG"* IN GERMAN, WHICH IN ENGLISH IS FREQUENTLY (MIS-) TRANSLATED MORE SIMPLISTICALLY AS *"IDEA".*

GEORG SAID...

...THE WORLD-- *NATURE*--IS THE EXTERNAL/ *CORPOREAL* FORM (ANTITHESIS) OF THE *IDEA* (SYNTHESIS)!

THE SYNTHESIS OF *IDEA* AND *NATURE* IS *GEIST* ("SPIRIT" OR "*MIND*"), A RATHER *SLIPPERY* CONCEPT THAT APPEARS TO BE TO HUMAN *BEHAVIOR* WHAT "*BEING*" IS TO GEORG'S *METAPHYSICS*:

A STATE OF HIGHEST *ABSTRACTION* IN "THE REALM OF *FREEDOM*."

JUST AS INDIVIDUAL *THINGS* EMANATE FROM FORMLESS *BEING*, SO INDIVIDUAL MOMENTS IN *HISTORY* EMANATE FROM *SPIRIT*.

AND JUST AS THE ABSOLUTE IDEA IS IN A NEVER-ENDING PROCESS OF *ACTUALIZATION*, HISTORY ITSELF IS IN A NEVER-ENDING FORWARD *ADVANCEMENT* TOWARD PERFECT EXPRESSION IN *ABSOLUTE SPIRIT*!

IN *RELIGION*, FOR EXAMPLE, WE BEGAN WITH AMORPHOUS *ANIMISM* (THESIS), WHICH MOVED TO PAGAN *ANTHROPOMORPHISM* (ANTITHESIS) -- IN WHICH *SPECIFIC* DEITIES EMBODY *SPECIFIC* ASPECTS OF CREATION -- CULMINATING IN *CHRISTIANITY* (SYNTHESIS), IN WHICH *ALL* OF CREATION IS EMBODIED IN ONE, *INDIVIDUAL* DEITY!

LIKEWISE, THE *STATE*, IN GEORG'S VIEW, IS *NOT* CREATED BY MAN, BUT EMANATES FROM DIALECTIC MOVEMENTS OF *HISTORY*!

"THE STATE IS THE *ACTUALITY* OF THE *ETHICAL IDEA*," HE WROTE, AN *ORGANISM* STRIVING TOWARD *MAXIMUM FREEDOM*.

AND SO IT MOVED FROM *TYRANNY* (THESIS) TO *DEMOCRACY* (ANTITHESIS) TO EUROPEAN-STYLE *MONARCHY* (SYNTHESIS)!

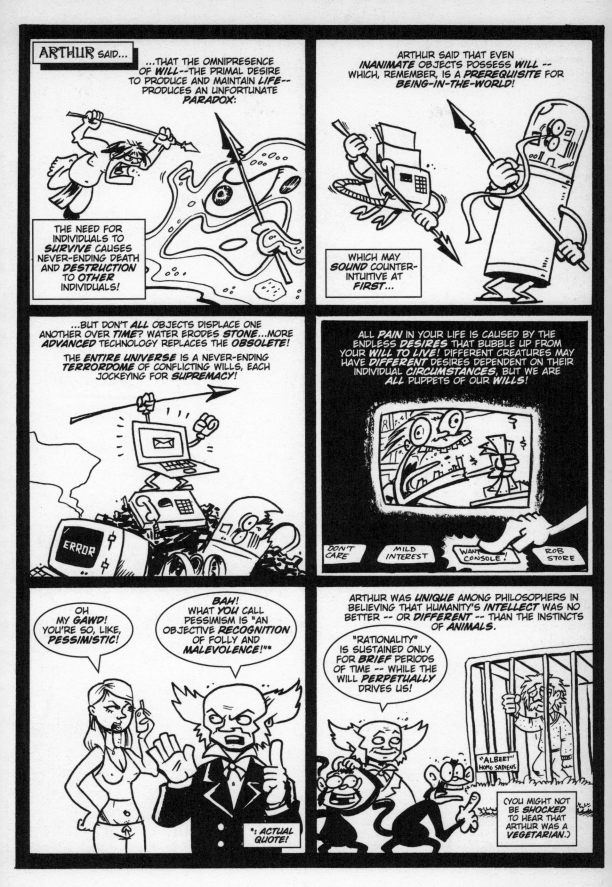

ARTHUR SAID...

...THAT THE OMNIPRESENCE OF *WILL*--THE PRIMAL DESIRE TO PRODUCE AND MAINTAIN *LIFE*-- PRODUCES AN UNFORTUNATE *PARADOX*:

THE NEED FOR INDIVIDUALS TO *SURVIVE* CAUSES NEVER-ENDING DEATH AND *DESTRUCTION* TO *OTHER* INDIVIDUALS!

ARTHUR SAID THAT EVEN *INANIMATE* OBJECTS POSSESS *WILL* -- WHICH, REMEMBER, IS A *PREREQUISITE* FOR *BEING-IN-THE-WORLD!*

WHICH MAY *SOUND* COUNTER-INTUITIVE AT *FIRST*...

...BUT DON'T *ALL* OBJECTS DISPLACE ONE ANOTHER OVER *TIME*? WATER ERODES *STONE*...MORE *ADVANCED* TECHNOLOGY REPLACES THE *OBSOLETE!*

THE *ENTIRE UNIVERSE* IS A NEVER-ENDING *TERRORDOME* OF CONFLICTING WILLS, EACH JOCKEYING FOR *SUPREMACY!*

ERROR

ALL *PAIN* IN YOUR LIFE IS CAUSED BY THE ENDLESS *DESIRES* THAT BUBBLE UP FROM YOUR *WILL TO LIVE!* DIFFERENT CREATURES MAY HAVE *DIFFERENT* DESIRES DEPENDENT ON THEIR INDIVIDUAL *CIRCUMSTANCES*, BUT WE ARE *ALL* PUPPETS OF OUR *WILLS!*

DON'T CARE | MILD INTEREST | WANT CONSOLE! | ROB STORE

OH MY GAWD! YOU'RE SO, LIKE, *PESSIMISTIC!*

BAH! WHAT *YOU* CALL PESSIMISM IS "AN OBJECTIVE *RECOGNITION* OF FOLLY AND *MALEVOLENCE!*"*

*: ACTUAL QUOTE!

ARTHUR WAS *UNIQUE* AMONG PHILOSOPHERS IN BELIEVING THAT HUMANITY'S *INTELLECT* WAS NO BETTER -- OR *DIFFERENT* -- THAN THE INSTINCTS OF *ANIMALS*.

"RATIONALITY" IS SUSTAINED ONLY FOR *BRIEF* PERIODS OF TIME -- WHILE THE WILL *PERPETUALLY* DRIVES US!

"ALBERT" HOMO SAPIENS

(YOU MIGHT NOT BE *SHOCKED* TO HEAR THAT ARTHUR WAS A *VEGETARIAN*.)

58

...IN *PART*, ONE MUST ASSUME, BECAUSE BERLIN U. SCHEDULED THEIR LECTURES FOR THE *EXACT SAME TIME*!

ARTHUR DIDN'T APPRECIATE THAT TOO MUCH:

"IF I WERE TO SAY THAT THE SO-CALLED *PHILOSOPHY* OF THIS FELLOW *HEGEL* IS A COLOSSAL PIECE OF *MYSTIFICATION*"...

THE HA-HA HOLE

"...WITH AN INEXHAUSTIBLE THEME FOR *LAUGHTER* AT OUR TIMES, THAT IT IS A *PSEUDO*-PHILOSOPHY *PARALYZING* ALL MENTAL POWERS, STIFLING ALL *REAL* THINKING..."

"...I SHOULD BE *QUITE RIGHT*!"*

"*FURTHER*, IF I WERE TO SAY THAT THIS *SUMMUS PHILOSOPHUS* SCRIBBLED *NONSENSE* QUITE UNLIKE *ANY* MORTAL *BEFORE* HIM..."

ASYLUM

"SO THAT WHOEVER COULD READ HIM WITHOUT FEELING AS IF HE WERE IN A *MADHOUSE*, WOULD QUALIFY AS AN INMATE FOR *BEDLAM*, I SHOULD BE NO *LESS* RIGHT!"*

"THE HEIGHT OF *AUDACITY* IN ... STRINGING TOGETHER SENSELESS AND EXTRAVAGANT *MAZES* OF WORDS...WAS FINALLY REACHED IN *HEGEL*...WITH A RESULT WHICH WILL APPEAR *FABULOUS* TO POSTERITY..."

"...AS A *MONUMENT* TO GERMAN *STUPIDITY*!"*

DUMMHEIT

"OUT OF EVERY *PAGE* OF *HUME'S* THERE IS MORE TO BE LEARNED THAN OUT OF *ALL* OF THE PHILOSOPHICAL WORKS OF *HEGEL*!"*

(*: ALL ACTUAL QUOTES, NATCH.)

HEGEL

AS FOR WHAT *GEORG* THOUGHT ABOUT *ARTHUR*...

UM...

ARTHUR *WHO*?

HE'S THE GUY WITH THE *FUNNY HAIR*, RIGHT...?

MUCH HAS BEEN MADE OF THE FACT THAT GEORG WAS ONE OF THE ONLY MAJOR PHILOSOPHERS SINCE ANCIENT TIMES TO ACTUALLY GET MARRIED.

THE STATE IS BUT THE SYNTHESIS OF THE FAMILY (THESIS) AND CIVIL SOCIETY (ANTITHESIS)!

ARTHUR SHUNNED HUMAN CONTACT AND SLEPT WITH A PISTOL.

HE WAS SO PARANOID HE DID ALL HIS OWN SHAVING BECAUSE "I WOULDN'T TRUST MY NECK TO ANOTHER MAN'S RAZOR."

GEORG WAS SO POPULAR, HIS FOLLOWERS SPLIT INTO CONSERVATIVE RIGHT HEGELIANS, WHO SUPPORTED THE PRUSSIAN MONARCHY...AND RADICAL LEFT HEGELIANS LIKE KARL MARX, WHO WANTED A REVOLUTIONARY SYNTHESIS OUT OF THE GOVERNMENTS OF THE PAST!

ARTHUR SAID THAT THE ONLY THREE CHARACTERS IN HISTORY WORTH KNOWING WERE BUDDHA, KANT, AND HIS PET POODLE.

"I FEEL MOST AT HOME AMONG DEMIGODS AND DOGS."

"THEY ALONE ARE FREE FROM THE FAILINGS OF MEN!"

CHIP

WHEN A CHOLERA EPIDEMIC SWEPT THROUGH BERLIN IN 1831, GEORG SUCCUMBED TO THE PLAGUE. SUPPOSEDLY HIS LAST WORDS WERE:

"ONLY ONE MAN EVER UNDERSTOOD ME."

"AND HE DIDN'T UNDERSTAND ME." ~GAK!~

BUT ARTHUR, WHO WAS TERRIFIED OF DISEASE, FLED THE CITY AS SOON AS THE PANDEMIC STARTED AND LIVED FOR ANOTHER THREE DECADES!

MY ASS IS OBJECTIFYING MY WILL TO GET THE HELL OUTTA HERE!

BERLIN

WHO GOT THE BETTER OF THE OTHER? YOU DECIDE!

60

Diogenes THE Cynic!

THE ROOT OF *"CYNIC"* IS THE GREEK *KUNIKOS*, OR *"DOGLIKE."*

HOW THIS PHILOSOPHER FROM SINOPES EARNED THAT APPELLATION IS NOT HARD TO *FIGURE OUT...*

DIOGENES BELIEVED THAT *NATURE*, NOT SOCIAL *CONVENTION*, SHOWED THE WAY TO A VIRTUOUS LIFE.

UNLIKE ANIMALS, THE ONLY LEASH A *WISE* MAN NEEDS TO POLICE HIS ACTION AND EXPRESSION IS HIS OWN *REASON!*

THE CYNICS HELD *ABSTRACT THINKING* IN CONTEMPT--ANY PHILOSOPHY WITH *VALUE* HAD TO BE *LIVED.*

AND THE KEY TO GOOD LIVING IS *SIMPLICITY*-- DIOGENES LIBERATED HIMSELF FROM THE OWNERSHIP OF ANY *POSSESSIONS.*

"HE HAS THE *MOST* WHO IS MOST CONTENT WITH THE *LEAST!"*

OBSERVING A *MOUSE* NEEDED NO REAL SHELTER, HE LIVED IN A BUSTED *PITHOS*, OR *TUB!*

HUMAN CUSTOMS *CONFUSE* NATURE'S PATH, SO DIOGENES *RIDICULED* TRADITION BY CONTINUOUSLY *FLAUNTING* HIS REPEATED VIOLATIONS OF THE SAME...

...DOING *EVERYTHING* IN PUBLIC, INCLUDING DRINKING, EATING (ETIQUETTE *NO-NO'S* IN ANCIENT ATHENS) AND EVEN *MASTURBATING* IN THE MARKETPLACE!

UGH! HE'S GOT NO MORE *SHAME* THAN A *STRAY DOG!*

HE ALSO KNEW HOW TO *BARK* AT HUMAN FOLLY...

PLEASE, ZEUS, LET ME BECOME *RICH* AND *FAMOUS...*

WOOF! WOOF!

HOW *DARE* YOU *INSULT* THE GODS ASKING FOR THINGS YOU *THINK* WILL MAKE YOU HAPPY...

...WHEN THEY HAVE *ALREADY* GIVEN YOU EVERYTHING YOU *NEED* FOR HAPPINESS?

YOU MAY *OPPOSE* BAD LUCK WITH *COURAGE*, BAD COMPANY WITH *NATURE*, AND BAD FEELINGS WITH *REASON!*

LAO TZU

MM MMOW MEH MAH ME MAMMH ME MAH ME MEMER-NAL MOW.*

MMO MMEH MMRE-EMEMM MEREM MERMPMP MOM MIM MMOW MEH MM1M MMOLIT MMOMMEM-MEM!*

*: "...THE TAO (CHINESE="PATH" OR "WAY") THAT CAN BE NAMED IS NOT THE ETERNAL TAO."

says...

*: "SO WE PRESENT THE FOLLOWING EXCEPTS FROM THIS LEGENDARY SAGE'S SPIRITUAL MASTERPIECE, THE TAO TE CHING ("THE BOOK OF THE WAY AND ITS VIRTUE," C. 600 B.C.), WITHOUT COMMENTARY!"

UNDER HEAVEN ALL CAN SEE BEAUTY AS BEAUTY ONLY BECAUSE THERE IS UGLINESS.

ALL CAN KNOW GOOD AS GOOD ONLY BECAUSE THERE IS EVIL.

THEREFORE HAVING AND NOT HAVING ARISE TOGETHER.

DIFFICULT AND EASY COMPLIMENT EACH OTHER.

THEREFORE, THE SAGE GOES ABOUT DOING NOTHING, TEACHING NO-TALKING.

WORK IS DONE, THEN FORGOTTEN.

THEREFORE, IT LASTS FOREVER.

WHY DO HEAVEN AND EARTH LAST FOREVER?

THEY ARE UNBORN, SO EVER LIVING.

DO YOU THINK YOU CAN IMPROVE THE UNIVERSE?

I DO NOT BELIEVE IT CAN BE DONE.

THE UNIVERSE IS SACRED. IF YOU TRY TO CHANGE IT, YOU WILL RUIN IT. IF YOU TRY TO HOLD IT, YOU WILL LOSE IT.

R.I.P.

CHIP

63

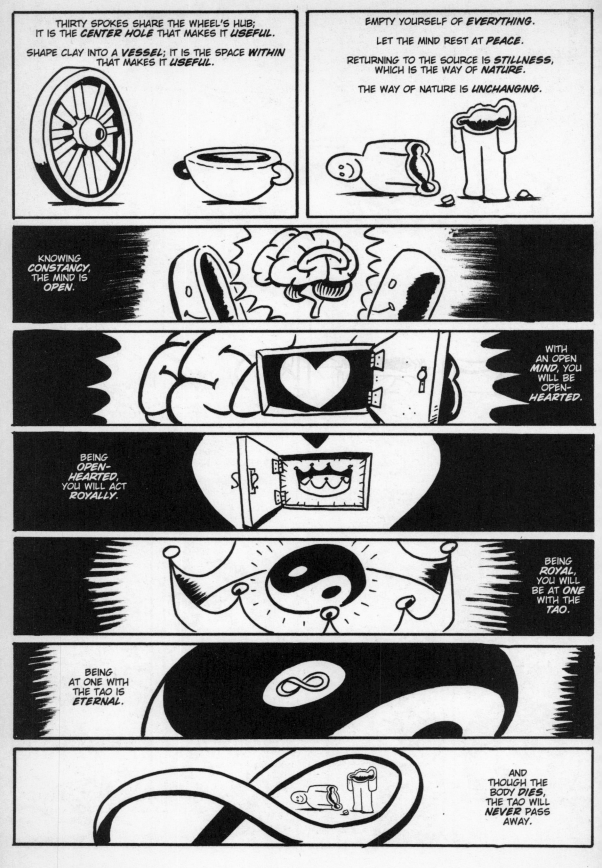

THIRTY SPOKES SHARE THE WHEEL'S HUB; IT IS THE *CENTER HOLE* THAT MAKES IT *USEFUL*.

SHAPE CLAY INTO A *VESSEL*; IT IS THE SPACE *WITHIN* THAT MAKES IT *USEFUL*.

EMPTY YOURSELF OF *EVERYTHING*.

LET THE MIND REST AT *PEACE*.

RETURNING TO THE SOURCE IS *STILLNESS*, WHICH IS THE WAY OF *NATURE*.

THE WAY OF NATURE IS *UNCHANGING*.

KNOWING *CONSTANCY*, THE MIND IS *OPEN*.

WITH AN OPEN *MIND*, YOU WILL BE OPEN-*HEARTED*.

BEING *OPEN-HEARTED*, YOU WILL ACT *ROYALLY*.

BEING *ROYAL*, YOU WILL BE AT *ONE* WITH THE *TAO*.

BEING AT ONE WITH THE TAO IS *ETERNAL*.

AND THOUGH THE BODY *DIES*, THE TAO WILL *NEVER* PASS AWAY.

THE FOUCAULT CIRCUS

The Birth of the Clinic, 1963

The Order of Things, 1966

SCIENCE LAB

Brothe

The History of Sexuality, 3 vols., 1976-1984

Madness and Civilization, 1961

ASYLUM

Archeology of Knowledge, 1969

SCHOOL

PRISON

Discipline and Punish, 1977

Michel Foucault (1926-1984) held a chair called "The History of Systems of Thought" at the *Collège de France*, which aptly sums up his life's work of systematically examining and critiquing the logical structure of social institutions.

"Why yes, my new book is called *Discipline & Punish*. How did you guess?"

66

Despite these institutions' claims of holding forth objective or essential knowledge, Foucault says, their assembled "truths" have in fact been subtly constructed by whatever elite happens to be in power at the time, to "reduce social agents to docile bodies" by forcing the powerless to unconsciously internalize the powerful's value system and structures of thought as their own. Furthermore, Foucault suggests that there is no knowledge other than what he calls "power-knowledge."

Not coincidentally, Foucault had some extreme ideas about social freedom, and garnered a reputation as something of a libertine: he was fond of anonymous gay S&M sex (which many believe contributed to his death from AIDS); he was once paid for a debate partially in hashish; and in 1977 he petitioned for France to abolish her age of consent laws (unsuccessfully).

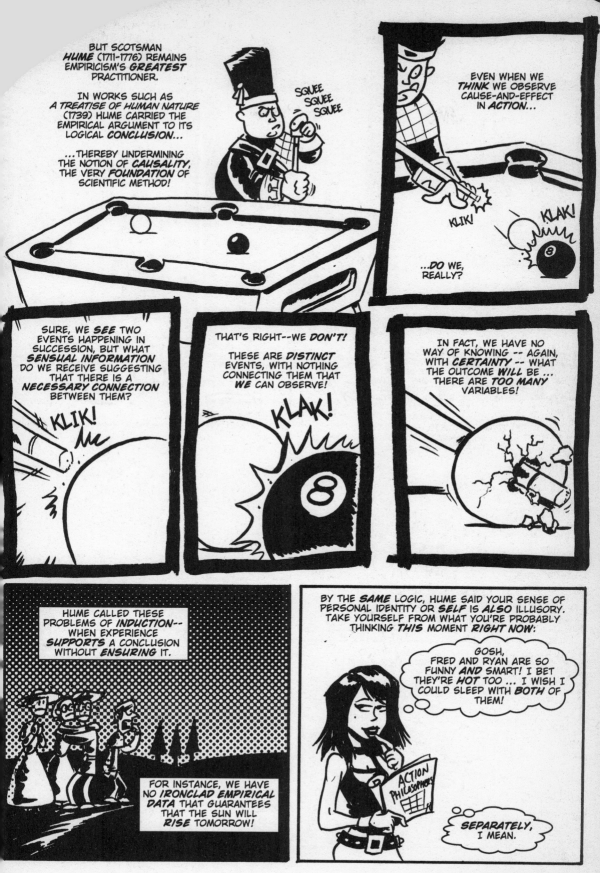

BUT SCOTSMAN *HUME* (1711-1776) REMAINS EMPIRICISM'S *GREATEST* PRACTITIONER.

IN WORKS SUCH AS *A TREATISE OF HUMAN NATURE* (1739) HUME CARRIED THE EMPIRICAL ARGUMENT TO ITS LOGICAL *CONCLUSION*...

...THEREBY UNDERMINING THE NOTION OF *CAUSALITY*, THE VERY *FOUNDATION* OF SCIENTIFIC METHOD!

SQUEE SQUEE SQUEE

EVEN WHEN WE *THINK* WE OBSERVE CAUSE-AND-EFFECT IN *ACTION*...

...DO WE, REALLY?

KLIK!

KLAK!

8

SURE, WE *SEE* TWO EVENTS HAPPENING IN SUCCESSION, BUT WHAT *SENSUAL INFORMATION* DO WE RECEIVE SUGGESTING THAT THERE IS A *NECESSARY CONNECTION* BETWEEN THEM?

KLIK!

THAT'S RIGHT--WE *DON'T!*

THESE ARE *DISTINCT* EVENTS, WITH NOTHING CONNECTING THEM THAT *WE* CAN OBSERVE!

KLAK!

8

IN FACT, WE HAVE NO WAY OF KNOWING -- AGAIN, WITH *CERTAINTY* -- WHAT THE OUTCOME *WILL* BE ... THERE ARE *TOO MANY* VARIABLES!

HUME CALLED THESE PROBLEMS OF *INDUCTION*-- WHEN EXPERIENCE *SUPPORTS* A CONCLUSION WITHOUT *ENSURING* IT.

FOR INSTANCE, WE HAVE NO *IRONCLAD EMPIRICAL DATA* THAT GUARANTEES THAT THE SUN WILL *RISE* TOMORROW!

BY THE *SAME* LOGIC, HUME SAID YOUR SENSE OF PERSONAL IDENTITY OR *SELF* IS *ALSO* ILLUSORY. TAKE YOURSELF FROM WHAT YOU'RE PROBABLY THINKING *THIS* MOMENT *RIGHT NOW*:

GOSH, FRED AND RYAN ARE SO FUNNY *AND* SMART! I BET THEY'RE *HOT* TOO ... I WISH I COULD SLEEP WITH *BOTH* OF THEM!

ACTION PHILOSOPHERS

SEPARATELY, I MEAN.

"WHEN I ENTER MOST *INTIMATELY* INTO WHAT I CALL *MYSELF*," HUME WRITES, "I ALWAYS STUMBLE ON SOME PARTICULAR *PERCEPTION* OR OTHER, OF HEAT OR COLD, LOVE OR HATRED, PAIN OR PLEASURE. I NEVER CAN CATCH *MYSELF* AT ANY TIME *WITHOUT* A PERCEPTION AND NEVER CAN OBSERVE ANYTHING *BUT* THE PERCEPTION."

IN OTHER WORDS, OUR ALLEGED *IDENTITIES* ARE NOTHING MORE THAN THE SUM OF THE *PERCEPTIONS* WE'VE ACCUMULATED -- IT IS ONLY THAT "HABIT OF *ASSOCIATION*" THAT CREATES CAUSE-AND-EFFECT THAT LEADS US TO BELIEV WE HAVE ONE *CONTINUOUS SELF* -- THAT WE ARE THE *SAME PERSON* IN *EACH* OF THE MOMENTS OF OUR LIVES!

BUT THIS INABILITY FOR US TO KNOW ANYTHING OUTSIDE *OURSELVES* SHOULDN'T MAKE YOU THINK HUME ADVOCATES *MORAL RELATIVISM.*

25¢

PLEASE HELP GOD BLESS

NO, FOR HUME, *MORALITY* HAS NOTHING TO DO WITH *REASON*-- RATHER, IT IS THE FACULTY OF *SYMPATHY* THAT GUIDES THE *RIGHT-NESS* OF OUR ACTIONS!

"IT IS NEEDLESS TO PUSH OUR RESEARCHES SO FAR AS TO ASK, *WHY* WE HAVE HUMANITY OR A FELLOW-FEELING WITH OTHERS," HUME WROTE. "IT IS SUFFICIENT, THAT THIS IS *EXPERIENCED* TO BE A *PRINCIPLE* OF HUMAN NATURE."

PLEASE HELP GOD BLESS

SYMPATHY MAKES US FEEL *GOOD* WHEN WE DO GOOD THINGS--BAD OR *GUILTY* WHEN WE DO *BAD* THINGS!

INDEED, HUME CONCLUDES, "REASON IS AND *OUGHT* TO BE THE SLAVE OF THE *PASSIONS.*" PERHAPS THIS IS WHY HUME'S *NICKNAME* AMONG HIS CONTEMPORARIES WAS *LE BON DAVID.*

NT LK WALK

"IN ALL MY LIFE, DID I NEVER MEET WITH A BEING OF A MORE *PLACID* AND *GENTLE* NATURE," A CRITIC OF THE DAY WROTE, "AND IT IS THIS *AMIABLE* TURN OF HIS CHARACTER, THAT HAS GIVEN MORE CONSEQUENCE AND *FORCE* TO HIS SKEPTICISM, THAN ALL THE ARGUMENTS OF HIS *SOPHISTRY.*"

WE ARE RESCUED FROM ANY *PESSIMISM* ABOUT REASON'S LIMITS BY A KIND OF BENIGN *ATTENTION DEFICIT DISORDER:*

"I *DINE,* I PLAY A GAME OF *BACKGAMMON,* I CONVERSE AND AM MERRY WITH MY *FRIENDS...*"

"...AND WHEN AFTER THREE OR FOUR HOURS' AMUSEMENT I WOULD RETURN TO THESE *SPECULATIONS...*"

"...THEY APPEAR SO COLD, SO STRAINED, AND *RIDICULOUS* THAT I CANNOT FIND IT IN MY HEART TO ENTER INTO THEM ANY *FURTHER!*"

IN OTHER WORDS, ANY CONTEMPLATION OF REASON'S *LIMITS* IS JUST ONE MORE *PERCEPTION* TO BE ADDED TO THE *SUM* OF YOUR LIFE!

THOUGH KNOWN IN THE WEST AS *CONFUCIUS* (551-479 B.C.), THIS LEGENDARY CHINESE THINKER IS BETTER KNOWN IN HIS NATIVE LAND AS *KONGZI*, WHICH LITERALLY TRANSLATES TO...

MASTER KONG

WHAT LITTLE IS KNOWN OF CONFUCIUS'S LIFE SUGGESTS HE SERVED AS A *SHI*, OR MIDDLE-CLASS *RETAINER*, DURING CHINA'S "DAYS OF SPRING AND AUTUMN" (800-400 B.C.) ...

...WHEN PETTY *TRIBAL KINGS* WARRED OVER THE FRAGMENTS OF THE COLLAPSED *ZHOU* DYNASTY.

THESE *FEUDAL THUGS* WERE EAGER TO ADD LEGITIMACY AND RESPECTABILITY TO THEIR REIGNS BY LEARNING THE COURT ETIQUETTE AND DIPLOMATIC PROTOCOL OF THE *ZHOUS* FROM ITERANT SCHOLARS LIKE CONFUCIUS.

CONFUCIUS'S TEACHINGS WERE COLLECTED IN THE *"FIVE CLASSICS"*, WHICH ULTIMATELY BECAME THE NATIONAL STANDARD OF TRADITIONAL *CHINESE ETHICS.*

AS EARLY AS 136 B.C., THE *FIVE CLASSICS* WERE *MANDATORY* READING FOR *ALL* WOULD-BE CIVIL SERVANTS.

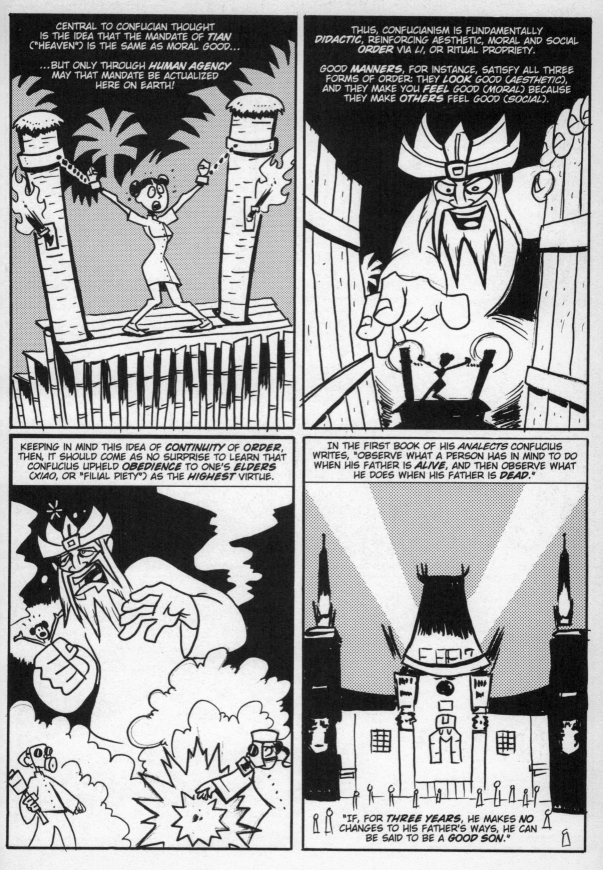

CENTRAL TO CONFUCIAN THOUGHT IS THE IDEA THAT THE MANDATE OF *TIAN* ("HEAVEN") IS THE SAME AS MORAL GOOD...

...BUT ONLY THROUGH *HUMAN AGENCY* MAY THAT MANDATE BE ACTUALIZED HERE ON EARTH!

THUS, CONFUCIANISM IS FUNDAMENTALLY *DIDACTIC*, REINFORCING AESTHETIC, MORAL AND SOCIAL *ORDER* VIA *LI*, OR RITUAL PROPRIETY.

GOOD *MANNERS*, FOR INSTANCE, SATISFY ALL THREE FORMS OF ORDER: THEY *LOOK* GOOD (AESTHETIC), AND THEY MAKE YOU *FEEL* GOOD (MORAL) BECAUSE THEY MAKE *OTHERS* FEEL GOOD (SOCIAL).

KEEPING IN MIND THIS IDEA OF *CONTINUITY* OF *ORDER*, THEN, IT SHOULD COME AS NO SURPRISE TO LEARN THAT CONFUCIUS UPHELD *OBEDIENCE* TO ONE'S *ELDERS* (XIAO, OR "FILIAL PIETY") AS THE *HIGHEST* VIRTUE.

IN THE FIRST BOOK OF HIS *ANALECTS* CONFUCIUS WRITES, "OBSERVE WHAT A PERSON HAS IN MIND TO DO WHEN HIS FATHER IS *ALIVE*, AND THEN OBSERVE WHAT HE DOES WHEN HIS FATHER IS *DEAD*."

"IF, FOR *THREE YEARS*, HE MAKES *NO* CHANGES TO HIS FATHER'S WAYS, HE CAN BE SAID TO BE A *GOOD SON*."

THERE'S A *TRICKLE-DOWN* EFFECT TO ALL THIS FILIAL PIETY: A GOOD SON WILL BE A GOOD FATHER AND LIKEWISE RAISE A GOOD SON.

A GOOD *MONARCH* WILL ALLOW HIS *GOODNESS* TO FLOW OUT TO HIS *SUBJECTS.*

THUS *MORAL FORCE (DE)* IS CONTAGIOUS.

THE *"PROFOUND MAN" (JUNZI)* EXERTS *DE,* THEREFORE MANIFESTS *VIRTUE (JEN),* THEREFORE FULFILLS *TIAN:*

"THE PROFOUND MAN ... DOES NOT SET HIS MIND EITHER FOR ANYTHING, OR AGAINST ANYTHING; WHAT IS RIGHT HE WILL FOLLOW," WRITES CONFUCIUS.

BUT THE *XIAOREN,* THE *SMALL MAN,* HE'S NOT WITH THE PROGRAM:

"THE PROFOUND MAN UNDER-STANDS WHAT IS MORAL; THE SMALL MAN UNDERSTANDS WHAT IS PROFITABLE." (ANALECTS 4:16)

"WHAT THE PROFOUND MAN SEEKS IS IN HIMSELF. WHAT THE SMALL MAN SEEKS IS IN OTHERS." (15:20)

SO WHAT'S THE *MORAL* OF MASTER KONG'S STORY? THAT'S RIGHT:

THE SMALL MAN *SUCKS.*

78

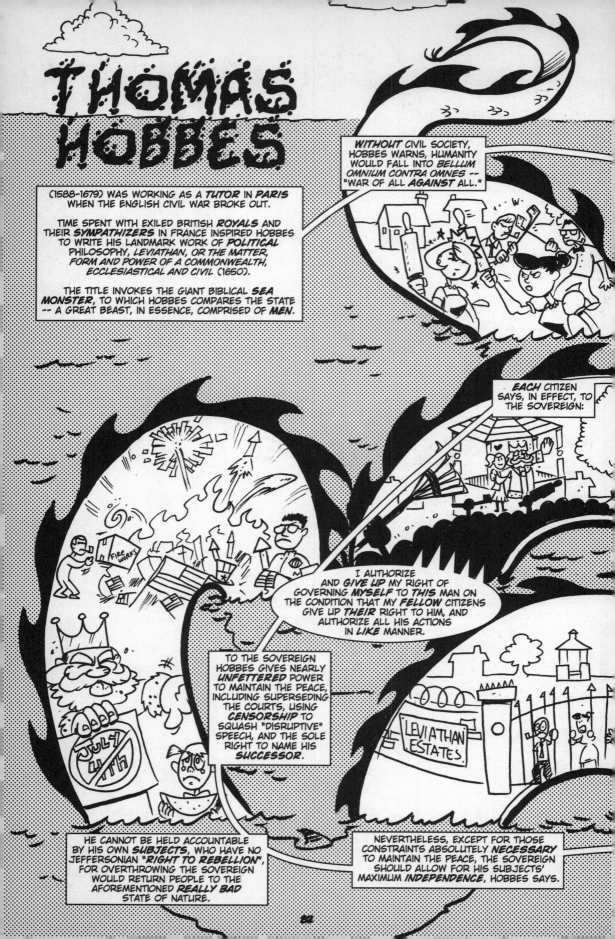

IN THIS WOEFUL "STATE OF *NATURE*", "EVERY MAN HAS A RIGHT TO *EVERY* THING, EVEN TO ONE ANOTHER'S *BODY*"-- WHICH WOULD MAKE A MAN'S LIFE "SOLITARY, POOR, NASTY, BRUTISH, AND *SHORT*."

TO OBTAIN *SECURITY* AGAINST CONSTANT VIOLENCE TO ONE'S PERSON, EACH MAN AGREES TO A *SOCIAL CONTRACT* ... HE *GIVES UP* THE IMMEDIATE GRATIFICATION OF ALL HIS *DESIRES* (WHICH BRING HIM INTO CONFLICT AND WITH OTHER MEN, THUS *SPARKING* VIOLENCE).

AND TO THE *STATE* HE GIVES A *MONOPOLY* ON THE JUST USE OF *FORCE*.

POLICE ARE ALLOWED TO USE VIOLENCE TO KEEP THE PEACE AMONG *CITIZENS*...

...AND WHEN *ANOTHER* STATE VIOLATES AGREE-MENTS WITH *OUR* STATE, THE *ARMY* IS ALLOWED TO USE VIOLENCE AGAINST *IT*.

UNFORTUNATELY, AS THERE IS NO APPEAL TO AN EARTHLY POWER *HIGHER* THAN THE SOVEREIGN, CITIZENS ARE ENTIRELY DEPENDANT ON THE SOVEREIGN'S OWN *GOODNESS* (OR LACK THEREOF) FOR HIM TO ADHERE TO THIS PRINCIPLE.

IRONICALLY, HOBBES' ROYALIST BUDDIES *DESPISED* LEVIATHAN BECAUSE THEY THOUGHT IT WAS EXCESSIVELY *SECULAR*. AFTER THEY THREATENED HIS *LIFE* HE HAD TO FLEE TO ENGLAND AND PETITION THE REBEL *CROMWELLIANS* FOR SANCTUARY!

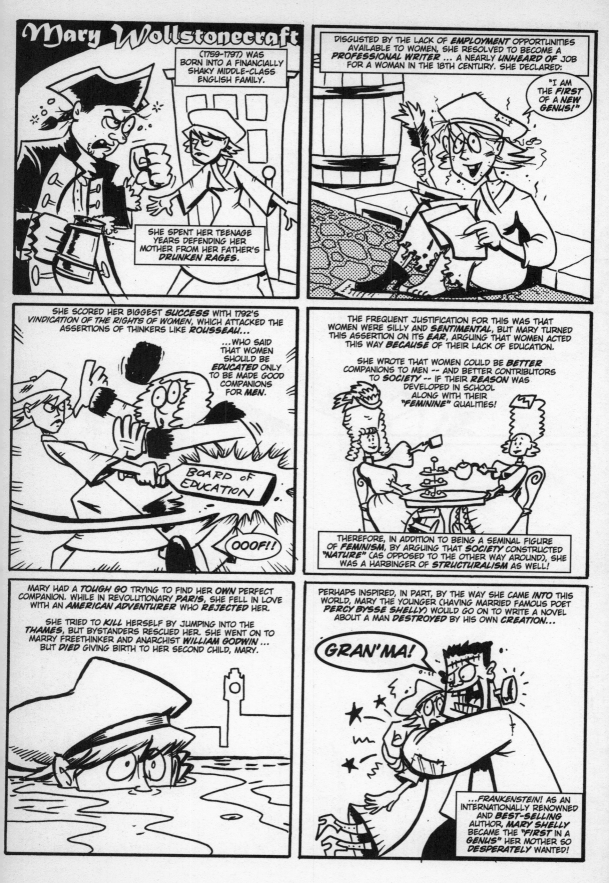

Mary Wollstonecraft

(1759-1797) WAS BORN INTO A FINANCIALLY SHAKY MIDDLE-CLASS ENGLISH FAMILY.

SHE SPENT HER TEENAGE YEARS DEFENDING HER MOTHER FROM HER FATHER'S *DRUNKEN RAGES.*

DISGUSTED BY THE LACK OF *EMPLOYMENT* OPPORTUNITIES AVAILABLE TO WOMEN, SHE RESOLVED TO BECOME A *PROFESSIONAL WRITER* ... A NEARLY *UNHEARD OF* JOB FOR A WOMAN IN THE 18TH CENTURY. SHE DECLARED:

"I AM THE *FIRST* OF A *NEW GENUS!*"

SHE SCORED HER BIGGEST *SUCCESS* WITH 1792'S *VINDICATION OF THE RIGHTS OF WOMEN,* WHICH ATTACKED THE ASSERTIONS OF THINKERS LIKE *ROUSSEAU* ...

...WHO SAID THAT WOMEN SHOULD BE *EDUCATED* ONLY TO BE MADE GOOD COMPANIONS FOR *MEN.*

BOARD of EDUCATION

OOOF!!

THE FREQUENT JUSTIFICATION FOR THIS WAS THAT WOMEN WERE SILLY AND *SENTIMENTAL,* BUT MARY TURNED THIS ASSERTION ON ITS *EAR,* ARGUING THAT WOMEN ACTED THIS WAY *BECAUSE* OF THEIR LACK OF EDUCATION.

SHE WROTE THAT WOMEN COULD BE *BETTER* COMPANIONS TO MEN -- AND BETTER CONTRIBUTORS TO *SOCIETY* -- IF THEIR *REASON* WAS DEVELOPED IN SCHOOL ALONG WITH THEIR *"FEMININE"* QUALITIES!

THEREFORE, IN ADDITION TO BEING A SEMINAL FIGURE OF *FEMINISM,* BY ARGUING THAT *SOCIETY* CONSTRUCTED *"NATURE"* (AS OPPOSED TO THE OTHER WAY AROUND), SHE WAS A HARBINGER OF *STRUCTURALISM* AS WELL!

MARY HAD A *TOUGH GO* TRYING TO FIND HER *OWN* PERFECT COMPANION. WHILE IN REVOLUTIONARY *PARIS,* SHE FELL IN LOVE WITH AN *AMERICAN ADVENTURER* WHO *REJECTED* HER.

SHE TRIED TO *KILL* HERSELF BY JUMPING INTO THE *THAMES,* BUT BYSTANDERS RESCUED HER. SHE WENT ON TO MARRY FREETHINKER AND ANARCHIST *WILLIAM GODWIN* ... BUT *DIED* GIVING BIRTH TO HER SECOND CHILD, MARY.

PERHAPS INSPIRED, IN PART, BY THE WAY SHE CAME *INTO* THIS WORLD, MARY THE YOUNGER (HAVING MARRIED FAMOUS POET *PERCY BYSSE SHELLY*) WOULD GO ON TO WRITE A NOVEL ABOUT A MAN *DESTROYED* BY HIS OWN *CREATION*...

GRAN'MA!

...FRANKENSTEIN! AS AN INTERNATIONALLY RENOWNED AND *BEST-SELLING* AUTHOR, *MARY SHELLY* BECAME THE *"FIRST IN A GENUS"* HER MOTHER SO *DESPERATELY* WANTED!

84

SPINOZA SPOKE OF OTHER *HERETICAL* THINGS -- THAT THE EXISTENCE OF *ANGELS* AND OTHER SPIRITS AND THE IMMORTALITY OF THE *SOUL* CANNOT BE JUSTIFIED BY *SCRIPTURE.*

HE REALIZED HE *OVER*SPOKE WHEN AN UNKNOWN ASSASSIN TRIED TO *STAB* HIM AS HE LEFT TEMPLE!

BENTO *KEPT* THE COAT FROM THAT DAY WITH HIM, TEAR AND ALL...

...PERHAPS TO REMIND HIM THAT THE LIFE OF THE *MIND* IS NOT ALWAYS THE *PEACEFUL* LIFE!

DUTCH JEWS WERE IN AN *ODD* POSITION IN THE MID-1600'S. HOLLAND HAD AGREED TO TAKE THEM IN AFTER SPAIN'S *KING FERDINAND* EXPELLED THEM FROM THE IBERIAN PENINSULA (SPINOZA'S FAMILY WAS ETHNICALLY *PORTUGUESE*) ONLY SO LONG AS THEY DIDN'T STIR UP *RELIGIOUS* TROUBLE.

EUROPEAN *CHRISTIANS* HAD ENOUGH PROBLEMS OF THEIR *OWN* WITH THE BLOODY PROTESTANT/ CATHOLIC SCHISM WITHOUT SHOULDERING THE BLASPHEMIES OF *OTHER* FAITHS.

AMSTERDAM'S RABBIS HAD ASSUMED THAT, AS SPINOZA WAS SUCH A *LEARNED* YOUTH, HE WAS ALSO *PIOUS.*

WAAA! BENTO SAID WE'RE NOT *IMMORTAL!*

AND HE DOUBTS MOSES WROTE THE WHOLE *TORAH!* WAAA!

HIS *ENEMIES* SOON CONVINCED THEM *OTHERWISE.*

HAULED BEFORE THE LEADERS OF DUTCH JEWRY, SPINOZA WAS OFFERED THE AWESOME SUM OF *ONE THOUSAND GUILDERS* TO PUBLICLY *RECANT.*

HIS *REPLY?*

"IN RETURN FOR THE TROUBLE YOU HAVE TAKEN TO TEACH ME THE *HEBREW LANGUAGE,* I AM QUITE WILLING TO SHOW YOU HOW TO *EXCOMMUNICATE ME.*"*

*: ACTUAL QUOTE!

86

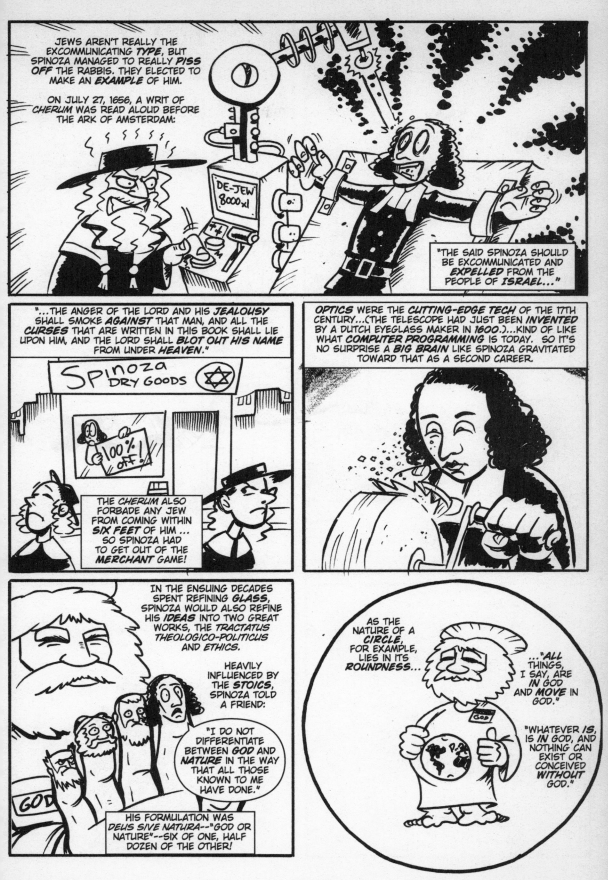

JEWS AREN'T REALLY THE EXCOMMUNICATING *TYPE*, BUT SPINOZA MANAGED TO REALLY *PISS OFF* THE RABBIS. THEY ELECTED TO MAKE AN *EXAMPLE* OF HIM.

ON JULY 27, 1656, A WRIT OF *CHERUM* WAS READ ALOUD BEFORE THE ARK OF AMSTERDAM:

DE-JEW 8000-xl

"THE SAID SPINOZA SHOULD BE EXCOMMUNICATED AND *EXPELLED* FROM THE PEOPLE OF *ISRAEL*..."

"...THE ANGER OF THE LORD AND HIS *JEALOUSY* SHALL SMOKE *AGAINST* THAT MAN, AND ALL THE *CURSES* THAT ARE WRITTEN IN THIS BOOK SHALL LIE UPON HIM, AND THE LORD SHALL *BLOT OUT HIS NAME* FROM UNDER *HEAVEN*."

Spinoza DRY GOODS

100% OFF!

THE *CHERUM* ALSO FORBADE ANY JEW FROM COMING WITHIN *SIX FEET* OF HIM ... SO SPINOZA HAD TO GET OUT OF THE *MERCHANT* GAME!

OPTICS WERE THE *CUTTING-EDGE TECH* OF THE 17TH CENTURY...(THE TELESCOPE HAD JUST BEEN *INVENTED* BY A DUTCH EYEGLASS MAKER IN *1600*.)...KIND OF LIKE WHAT *COMPUTER PROGRAMMING* IS TODAY. SO IT'S NO SURPRISE A *BIG BRAIN* LIKE SPINOZA GRAVITATED TOWARD THAT AS A SECOND CAREER.

IN THE ENSUING DECADES SPENT REFINING *GLASS*, SPINOZA WOULD ALSO REFINE HIS *IDEAS* INTO TWO GREAT WORKS, THE *TRACTATUS THEOLOGICO-POLITICUS* AND *ETHICS*.

HEAVILY INFLUENCED BY THE *STOICS*, SPINOZA TOLD A FRIEND:

"I DO NOT DIFFERENTIATE BETWEEN *GOD* AND *NATURE* IN THE WAY THAT ALL THOSE KNOWN TO ME HAVE DONE."

GOD

HIS FORMULATION WAS *DEUS SIVE NATURA*--"GOD OR NATURE"--SIX OF ONE, HALF DOZEN OF THE OTHER!

AS THE NATURE OF A *CIRCLE*, FOR EXAMPLE, LIES IN ITS *ROUNDNESS*...

GOD

..."*ALL* THINGS, I SAY, ARE *IN* GOD AND *MOVE* IN GOD."

"WHATEVER *IS*, IS *IN* GOD, AND NOTHING CAN EXIST OR CONCEIVED *WITHOUT* GOD."

WHAT DROVE THE RABBIS *NUTS* ABOUT SPINOZA WAS HIS INSISTENCE THAT GOD IS NOT A *TRANSITIVE* BUT RATHER AN *IMMANENT* CAUSE OF REALITY.

WRONG!

HELLO GOD

THIS VERY *ARISTOTELIAN* DISTINCTION SIMPLY MEANS THAT GOD IS NOT A *PERSONALITY*, OBJECTIVELY *"CREATING"* REALITY LIKE AN ARTISAN CRAFTS A *LENS*.

NO-- GOD CREATES REALITY BY *BEING* REALITY! SPINOZA: "GOD I UNDERSTAND TO BE A BEING ABSOLUTELY *INFINITE*, THAT IS, A SUBSTANCE CONSISTING OF INFINITE ATTRIBUTES, *EACH* OF WHICH EXPRESSES ETERNAL AND INFINITE *ESSENCE*."

NEW GOD

GOD Sr.

GODYEAR

GOD TIMES

EVERYTHING THAT *IS*, THEREFORE, IS MERELY A *"MODE"* OF GOD.

RIGHT!

NO *WONDER* SPINOZA'S FELLOW PHILOSOPHERS NICKNAMED HIM "THAT *GOD-INTOXICATED* MAN!"

AWRIGHT, BUDDY, YOU'RE *CUT OFF.*

AND JUST AS A CIRCLE *MUST* BE ROUND, SPINOZA WRITES, "THINGS COULD *NOT* HAVE BEEN PRODUCED BY GOD IN ANY MANNER OR IN ANY ORDER *DIFFERENT* FROM THAT WHICH IN FACT *EXISTS.*"

IN THIS WAY SPINOZA *DEMOLISHES* ARISTOTLE'S TWO MILLENNIA-HELD DISTINCTION BETWEEN *POSSIBILITY* AND *ACTUALITY*: IF SOMETHING *COULD* BE, IT *IS.* IF IT *CAN'T*, IT'S *NOT.*

Platypus Prototype Presentation

A   B   C

HMMM... SO HARD TO *DECIDE...*

SINCE *FREEDOM* IS NOTHING MORE THAN THE ABILITY TO ACT ACCORDING TO ONE'S OWN *NATURE*, GOD IS ALSO ABSOLUTELY *FREE.*

GOD

THEREFORE ... AND THIS IS WHY "THE MAN" *REALLY* CAN'T STAND SPINOZA ... SO ARE *WE*, WHO ARE *PART* OF GOD!

REASON'S **SECOND** ROLE IS TO LET US UNDERSTAND THE DIFFERENCE BETWEEN WHAT WE **CAN** AND **CANNOT** CONTROL, SO WE MIGHT NOT BE UNNECESSARILY **DISCOURAGED** BY THE **LATTER**.

THE PASSIONS ARE **POWERFUL**, HOWEVER, AND MERE REASON **ALONE** CANNOT HOPE TO STAND AGAINST THEM. ALL THE TIME WE FOOLISHLY "FOLLOW THE **WORSE** COURSE EVEN WHEN WE KNOW THE **BETTER**."

NO, WE NEED TO FIGHT EMOTION WITH ITS **EQUAL**-- REASON'S **OWN** PASSION, WHICH SPINOZA CALLS "THE **INTELLECTUAL** LOVE OF **GOD**."

UNLIKE **OUR** EMOTIONS, WHICH SO OFTEN ARE UTTERLY **DISPROPORTIONATE** TO THEIR OBJECTS, THE LOVE OF GOD IS WHOLLY "**ACCURATE**" (CONTROLLED, AS IT IS, BY **REASON**).

TO KNOW, KNOW, KNOW HIM IS TO LOVE, LOVE, LOVE HIM...

Tiger Beat

...AND I DO...

KNOWING GOD **IS** LOVING GOD, AND **VICE-VERSA**. AND IT IS THE GREATEST LOVE **POSSIBLE**, FOR, BECAUSE WE ARE **PART** OF GOD, OUR LOVE OF GOD IS **ALSO** GOD'S LOVE FOR **HIMSELF**. WHEN WE LOVE **OURSELVES**, WE LOVE THE **UNIVERSE**.

NOK! NOK! NOK!

BIG 'UNS

Kleenx

STAY OUT, MOM! I'M LOVIN' THE UNIVERSE!!

HOWEVER, SPINOZA WRITES, "IT **CANNOT** BE SAID THAT GOD **LOVES** MANKIND, MUCH LESS THAT HE **SHOULD** LOVE THEM BECAUSE **THEY** LOVE HIM, OR **HATE** THEM BECAUSE **THEY** HATE HIM."

--SIGH--... WILL HE EVER **NOTICE** ME?

"HE WHO LOVES GOD **CANNOT** ENDEAVOR THAT GOD SHOULD LOVE HIM IN **RETURN**."

SPINOZA'S GOD DOESN'T **DO** MIRACLES. HE DOESN'T ANSWER YOUR **PRAYERS**.

HE DOESN'T **WATCH** OVER YOU OR YOUR **LOVED ONES** ANY MORE THAN **YOU** SPEND ALL **YOUR** TIME WATCHING OVER DISTINCT PARTS OF YOUR **BODY**.

GOD

GOTTFRIED LEIBNIZ

(1646-1716), co-inventor (along with ISAAC NEWTON) of CALCULUS, believed that he had proven the existence of GOD through a rather complicated cosmology hinging upon the idea that the universe is made up of an infinite number of POINTS he called MONADS, each one of which had the entire universe imperfectly reflected in it, even as it was a distinct part of the WHOLE...

...WHICH MEANT, OF COURSE, THAT THERE MUST BE A GOD, FOR ONLY A PERFECT BEING COULD HAVE CONCEIVED OF SUCH AN ORDERLY UNIVERSE. (THOUGH SINCE LEIBNIZ CONCEIVED IT TOO, DOES THAT MAKE HIM PERFECT?)

AND, BECAUSE GOD IS PERFECT, HE CONSIDERED ALL THE WORLDS HE COULD HAVE BUILT, AND ENDED UP BUILDING THIS ONE. THEREFORE:

"WE LIVE IN THE BEST OF ALL POSSIBLE WORLDS!"

NOW, TO PARAPHRASE FOUR OF OUR FAVORITE PHILOSOPHERS, THE MARX BROTHERS: WHO ARE YOU GOING TO BELIEVE?

LEIBNIZ ... OR YOUR LYING EYES?

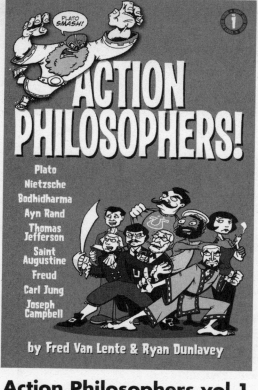
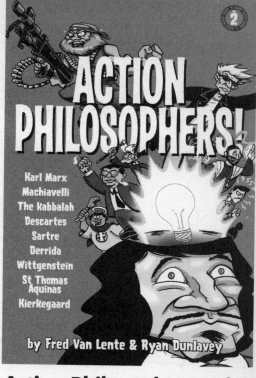

ABOUT THE CREATORS

FRED VAN LENTE (writer) dropped out of graduate school at the University of Pittsburgh so he could move to Brooklyn and write comic books. Fred's graphic novels include **Super-Villain Team-Up** (Marvel), **The Silencers** (Image/Moonstone) and **Tranquility** (winner of the Spectrum Award for: Best Science Fiction Art) and is the current writer of **Marvel Adventures Iron Man**. www.fredvanlente.com

RYAN DUNLAVEY (artist) recieved a C+ in Philosophy 101 at Syracuse University. He is a freelance illustrator based in New York City. Ryan's comics have appeared in **MAD, Wizard, ToyFare** and **Royal Flush**. www.ryandartist.com